INTENTIONAL FROM THE START

GUIDING EMERGENT READERS IN SMALL GROUPS

CAROLYN HELMERS

AND

SUSAN VINCENT

STENHOUSE PUBLISHERS

PORTSMOUTH, NEW HAMPSHIRE

Stenhouse Publishers
www.stenhouse.com

Credits
Figures 2.1b–2.1e, *The Sky* by Ann Staman © 2006 by School Specialty, LLC. Reproduced with permission.
Figures 2.1f–2.1j, *The Costume Party* by Ann Staman © 2006 by School Specialty, LLC Reproduced with permission.
Figures 2.2b–2.2f, *Love* by Ann Staman © 2006 by School Specialty, LLC. Reproduced with permission.
Figures 2.2g–2.2k, *Big House, Little Mouse* by Ann Staman © 2005 by School Specialty, LLC. Reproduced with permission.
Figures 2.3b–2.3f, *My Stuffed Animals* by Ann Staman © 2000 by School Specialty, LLC. Reproduced with permission.
Figures 2.3g–2.3k, *A Hot Day* by Ann Staman © 2005 by School Specialty, LLC. Reproduced with permission.
Figures 2.4b–2.4f, *Rabbit's Skating Party* by Ann Staman © 2005 by School Specialty, LLC. Reproduced with permission.
Figures 2.4g–2.4k, *The Roller Coaster* by Ann Staman © 2000 by School Specialty, LLC. Reproduced with permission.
Figure 4.4, *The Fence* by Ann Staman ©2006 by School Specialty, LLC. Reproduced with permission.
Figures 4.5a and 4.5b, *A Seed* by Ann Staman © 2007 by School Specialty, LLC. Reproduced with permission.
Figures 5.5 and 5.6, *A Bike for Russ* by Ann Staman © 2005 by School Specialty, LLC. Reproduced with permission.
Figure 5.19, *Little Mouse* by Ann Staman © 2000 by School Specialty, LLC. Reproduced with permission.
Figures 6.4, 6.5, and 6.7, *No, Bo!* by Ann Staman © 2000 by School Specialty, LLC. Reproduced with permission.

Library of Congress Cataloging-in-Publication Data

Names: Helmers, Carolyn, author. | Vincent, Susan, 1964– author.
Title: Intentional from the start : guiding emergent readers in small groups /
    Carolyn Helmers and Susan Vincent.
Description: Portsmouth, New Hampshire : Stenhouse Publishers, 2021. |
    Includes bibliographical references and index.
Identifiers: LCCN 2020054564 (print) | LCCN 2020054565 (ebook) |
    ISBN 9781625311948 (paperback) | ISBN 9781625311955 (ebook)
Subjects: LCSH: Reading (Early childhood) | Group reading.
Classification: LCC LB1139.5.R43 H45 2021 (print) | LCC LB1139.5.R43
    (ebook) | DDC 372.4—dc23
LC record available at https://lccn.loc.gov/2020054564
LC ebook record available at https://lccn.loc.gov/2020054565

Cover design, interior design, and typesetting by Progressive Publishing Services

Printed in the United States of America

This book is printed on paper certified by third-party standards for sustainably managed forestry.

25 24 23 22 21 20 19   4371   9 8 7 6 5 4 3 2 1

Dedication

For teachers and emergent readers
who work closely every day at the small-group table.

Contents

Foreword

Somehow, I knew this book would come into the world. Or maybe I only hoped that it would.

In September 1989, I walked into a first-grade classroom. *My* first-grade classroom. My *first* first-grade classroom. The school year had started a few weeks ago and my new school was now adding a section of first grade. I was beyond excited to be employed (and believe me, my parents were happy about that, too!), and not only that, I had landed my dream job: living and learning with kids every day.

As I stood in the doorway, I saw empty shelves, a faded bulletin board with clowns on it (not a fan), and a crusty Crockpot™ in the corner. It was not exactly what I had envisioned, yet with only a couple of days to get my classroom ready for students, I dug in and got to work. After all, I knew I wanted to be a teacher, I had graduated from a solid teacher-preparation program, and I knew what I believed about good instruction. The only thing left to do was teach.

My first year was tough. First years often are. Ups and downs, periods of utter frustration mixed with moments of unexpected, total joy. I made it through, and year one has turned into year thirty-one in the blink of an eye. What I know now is that sometimes, in the middle of the fray, when the G-force of the learning curve causes you to hold on for dear life, you need a guide, not a script, not a mandated set of rules to follow. What I also know now is that every single year of our teaching careers, if we're lucky, feels like that same learning curve all over again. We learn, we unlearn, we relearn. Scripts and mandates come and go, but guides help us grow. And that's where this book comes in.

Intentional from the Start is a guide for primary reading teachers, new or not-so-new, who realize that the little decisions they make every day, in this case with emergent readers, might be small but they are powerful. This book respects the prior knowledge we bring and helps us think deeply within the framework of small-group guided reading. The chapters take us from familiar, broad concepts like small-group instruction, leveled readers, and literacy work stations to a nuanced understanding of what actually happens at a small-group table with emergent readers.

Many primary teachers wonder: What are the in-the-moment teaching moves to consider when children are not yet responding to print? How might we guide emergent readers into a meaningful relationship with text, valuing their thinking from the very start? How can we use levels of text and not the other way around? Carolyn and Susan answer these questions here, their responses grounded in theory, yet with their practical wisdom shining through in every scenario.

There's something to know *before* you read—something you'll be sure to notice *as* you read. Carolyn and Susan have centered the reader over all else. The reader before text levels. The reader before predetermined instructional moves. Readers matter most, and our responses to readers in small groups are what this book is all about. Big thinking about small groups!

How did I know that this book would make its way into the world, or at least hope that it would? Because I have known the real, everyday work of Carolyn and Susan for years. I've had the honor of sitting in Carolyn's kindergarten classroom after the students have gone, listening to her reflect aloud and plan her next teaching moves. I've watched as Susan teaches teachers; her deep knowledge base and infectious enthusiasm make learning exciting. Two more earnest and experienced primary educators you may never find. This book has been percolating in these two practitioners' minds over time, and is now presented as a gift to teachers and their young readers everywhere.

Tanny McGregor
Cincinnati, Ohio

Acknowledgments

We are lucky to have started our teaching careers in the Forest Hills School District way back in 1991. They have always valued professional learning and have given us many opportunities to grow as reading teachers. We appreciate their investment in our learning by allowing us to become trained in Reading Recovery™ through The Ohio State University and sending us to annual literacy conferences. Their full support in sharing our ideas in this book is greatly appreciated. We would also like to thank the many, many Forest Hills School District colleagues who have collaborated and learned with us as well as supporting us on this new writing adventure.

We wish to extend a big thank you to our own mentors Bonnie Sickinger and Deborah Rudolph. They took us under their wings as we began our teaching careers and made sure we were on the right path to learning about and understanding emergent literacy. They taught us what it means to be life-long learners and to always put the child at the forefront as we planned our instruction.

We are forever grateful to the Reading Recovery™ learning community, which is where we first met. We continue to learn from the brilliance of Marie Clay and are grateful to those who helped us understand her work, especially Mary D. Fried, Gay Su Pinnell, Irene Fountas, and Jan Richardson. We would also like to thank all the Ohio Reading Recovery™ trainers, teacher leaders, and teachers (past and present) who have practiced intentional teaching every day.

Thank you to the supportive colleagues at Miami University. Thank you to EPS's Handprints books and Ann Staman Hollingworth and to Reading Reading books for allowing us to showcase their carefully crafted books, which scaffold emergent readers' growth. These books are well loved by both children and teachers.

Our deepest gratitude to our friend and mentor Tanny McGregor. We have been learning from you as a teacher and a person for many years. We love talking, listening, reading, writing, and sketch-noting with you. You are a gift to the teaching profession.

This book would never have been written if it weren't for our editor, Terry Thompson, popping into our presentation at the National Reading Recovery Conference. He has been a blessing since the start of this project. His guidance, kind words, support, and patience have helped us to see ourselves as writers who could share the important work we do with children. From the bottom of our hearts, thank you Terry! We couldn't have done it without you!

Our heartfelt gratitude goes out to the rest of our Stenhouse team, Shannon St. Peter and Stephanie Levy. Your hard work behind the scenes to get this book to print is greatly appreciated. Thank you also to Lynn Gohn for your consistently speedy work on design and production.

To our parents, Bill and Shirley and Joe and Sandy, thank you for being our very first teachers. You helped to nurture our own love of reading from early in our elementary school years and beyond. Your unconditional love and support have helped to shape the teachers we have become. We love you!

Of course, we can't forget our most loyal supporters, our families. From the beginning they believed in us and what we had to say. When we were overwhelmed, they reminded us to take a breath and then dig in again. Their willingness to be abandoned for hours at a time while we wrote, edited, and rewrote at our favorite restaurant is much appreciated. To our husbands, Ken and Troy, and our children Emily and her husband Zach, Tommy, Hannah and her husband Jacob, and Jonathan, thank you for your constant love and support! We love you!

Introduction: Learning from the Start

Years ago, when we started as novice teachers, we really had no idea how to teach 20 six-year-olds how to read. Lucky for us, we both had wonderful teammates who mentored us and generously shared everything they did—including a framework of activities to structure our days. Being new and inexperienced, we followed their frameworks and were glad to know *what* to do, even if we didn't really understand the *why* or the *how*. In the beginning, we were simply step-followers. And for a while that was okay. Step following is a great beginning for any complex process. You can get okay results from following steps. And that's exactly what we both got in those first few years of teaching—our kids did okay. Not great, but okay.

To get better than okay results, however, we needed to move beyond just following the steps of guided reading. The ideas we present in this book are grounded in theory and we want you to have an understanding of that theory to help you move beyond *doing* the steps of guided reading and toward making expert decisions about what the earliest readers need during that critical small-group time.

To begin making those expert decisions, we had to gain an understanding that children develop socially, emotionally, and academically on a wide continuum and certainly not all at the same time. Just as there is a *developmentally normal* range for babies to learn to sit, crawl, talk, and walk, there is a developmentally normal range for learning how to read and write. In our kindergarten and first-grade classrooms, some students walk through the door already reading, while others come to us eager to look at print and begin instruction. Still others enter our classrooms not knowing any letters and need a completely different early literacy experience to start their reading careers. This wide range of learners seen in every classroom is considered, in fact, developmentally normal. Just as a pediatrician must understand child development to be able to provide proper, appropriate care, it is our job as literacy teachers to be knowledgeable about emergent readers and be ready to meet them where they are in their reading development and build from there.

Both of us are extremely passionate about early literacy and teaching children. With more than fifty years of working with emergent readers between us, we've shared in many success stories and challenges while supporting our youngest learners as they begin their lifelong journey of becoming readers. Throughout those years, we've come to see and understand the need for a book with a narrow focus just like this. So many professional books about young readers are written for grades K-6 with very little information that actually applies to the five- and six-year-old learner. Whether students are normally developing kindergartners or early first graders or children in intervention programs who need extra support, we see the need to have stronger conversations that focus specifically on the literacy needs of our earliest learners.

Teaching children to read is not haphazard. We can't just teach the letters, teach the sounds, teach the words, and give books to children and expect they'll learn how to read. In reality, it's not that simple. Teaching children to read must include a well-thought-out plan with a repertoire of tools and strategies, so we can teach right at the edge of each child's zone of proximal development (Vygotsky and Cole 1981). With that in mind, we're big proponents of understanding the theory or the *why* behind the teaching decisions we make in our classrooms. Our goal in writing this book is to help you understand the *why* as well as the *how* of teaching reading in your small groups to your youngest learners.

So, we begin with a chapter on reading theory and research to help you understand how the brain undertakes the amazing task of becoming a reader. We'll also explore the role a child's emotions play in learning to read. As we move forward, we'll keep our focus in each chapter on small-group instruction and the emergent reader—what they need to learn at each step along the way, how to teach precisely what they need to know, and which tools might be useful.

We'll start with the learners who walk through the door not knowing how to write their names, let alone any letter names. The sense of urgency to assist these learners is always the greatest because, although developmentally normal, the gap between them and their peers needs to be narrowed quickly. From there we'll turn our focus to those learners who are ready to begin to look at print, so they can discover how print works and train their eyes how to consistently look from left to right at the sentence level and then the word level. While doing that, we'll give you strategies to firm up letter knowledge and introduce high frequency words to help learners begin to monitor their reading. And, in conjunction with all this reading work going on, we'll also focus on writing, because we firmly believe that reading and writing are reciprocal processes that develop side by side with good teaching.

In this book, we've chosen to focus our discussions on small-group, guided reading, because we believe in its power to motivate learners and help them develop a love of reading. As you work with four to six children in this setting for fifteen to twenty minutes a day, we'll show you how to differentiate instruction by integrating a variety of highly engaging texts with individualized support and feedback. Yes, we know you'll have to plan for multiple groups each week. Yes, we know small-group instruction takes more thoughtful planning on your part when it is based on what learners know and need to know next. Yes, we know you need to spend time getting to know lots of texts so you can utilize them well. Yes, yes, yes—we know all the yeses, but we argue the benefits make it all worthwhile!

However, though it will be our focus throughout this book, it's important to note that small-group reading instruction is a smaller piece of a much larger literacy puzzle (Figure I.1) for the emergent readers you teach. Exposing students to a wide variety of print in a wide variety of ways is crucial. To that end, we advocate for small-group, guided reading instruction in primary classrooms supported by an integrated, balanced program that engages children in the following:

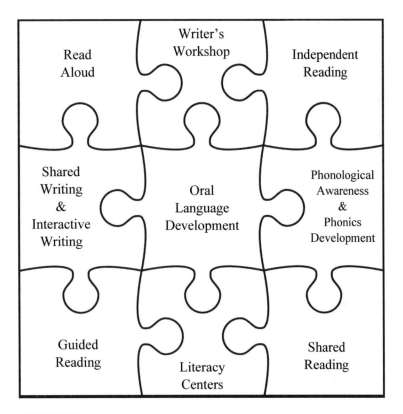

FIGURE I.1
Literacy Puzzle

- **Oral language development.** The foundation of all reading and writing activities is oral language. Students need to engage in social as well as academic conversations with adults and peers throughout the day. These conversations help young readers acquire new vocabulary that can help them make connections with school and home, as well as the world around them.
- **Phonological awareness and phonemic awareness.** Children need to spend a small amount of time each day developing the skill of recognizing, playing with and manipulating sounds in language (rhyming, blending/segmenting, isolating, adding/deleting/ substituting). This type of work is always oral and doesn't involve print.
- **Phonics.** Phonics is the relationship between the letters and the sounds they make. It is a foundational skill that is developed as children become writers and readers. With a skilled and knowledgeable teacher, children learn to encode (link letters to sounds) when writing and decode (link sounds to letters) when reading.
- **Read-alouds.** Strong literacy programs incorporate several read-alouds a day. Teachers gather their students on the floor and read books from a variety of genres. Read-alouds provide opportunities for students to hear fluent reading with good phrasing and intonation. The discussion that takes place before, during, and after reading the book aids in building oral language, vocabulary, and comprehension. However, there are times when a book should be read just because it's fun!

- **Shared reading.** During shared reading, students share in the responsibility of reading a text. The text may be a poem, chart, or a book, and the print should be large enough for the entire group to see. Often the text is reread over the course of a few days, which provides the perfect opportunity to model and teach concepts of print and problem-solving strategies.
- **Independent reading.** In a balanced literacy program, students will need plenty of opportunities to interact with a variety of books on their own. Emergent readers begin the year by using the pictures in trade books to "tell" and retell stories. With small-group, guided reading instruction they end the year reading emergent texts.
- **Shared writing.** Shared writing provides the opportunity for the class to craft a text together while the teacher does the writing. As the teacher writes, they teach and model text conventions (directionality, word spacing, punctuation, return sweep, and so on). The teacher also models writing known high frequency words fast and how to say unknown words slowly, listening for and linking sounds to letters. The result is always a text that can be read by all the students.
- **Interactive writing.** Interactive writing differs from shared writing only in that the students interact with the text alongside the teacher during the task of writing. Students and their teacher still craft the text together, but students write the parts that they know (letter or words) as the teacher writes the unknown parts. Again, the result is the same as shared writing, a text that can be read by everyone.
- **Writer's workshop.** Students need opportunities to write every day on topics they choose. Writer's workshop is the time to do this. It usually begins with a focused mini-lesson, then provides time for students to write independently and ends with a reflection on how the workshop went or students sharing their writing. Through this process, students at emergent levels learn first to convert oral stories to picture stories and later, learn to craft picture stories with words.
- **Literacy centers.** For good instruction to take place at the small-group table, the other students need engaging practice work to do. This can be executed with literacy centers (examples of centers include reading center, writing center, listening center, letters and sounds center, word center, and so on). Within each literacy center, there should be the opportunity for student choice. Choice allows students to decide how they want to practice what they have learned and helps them remain engaged for longer periods. For more on this, check out the companion resources for this book at www.stenhouse.com/content/intentional-from-the-start. There, you'll find plenty of ideas for how your literacy centers can directly support the learning taking place at your small-group table.

We hope as you read this book, you'll come to see that emergent learners have very important work to do at these earliest levels and it's not as easy as it seems. It takes a skilled conductor and a great deal of effort to orchestrate this important early learning. As we explore the *why* behind the learning so you can plan for the most appropriate *how*, we understand that despite the best-laid plans, most of your decisions will need to be made on the run. So, we'll give you lots of tools to make the most powerful choices for your young readers in the moment. And, by the end of this book, we trust that no matter what pressure comes down the pike, you'll be prepared to make the incredibly complicated process of teaching emergent readers to read, in fact, look easy!

Emergent Readers: How They Learn and How to Teach Them

It's late October in Mrs. Jones's kindergarten classroom. As you stroll through her classroom as a casual visitor you observe children hard at work during literacy centers. They are spread out through the room using every nook and cranny possible. Some are utilizing tables, others the floor, and still others choose some flexible seating options (under tables, standing at high tables, in beanbags, in scoop chairs, on yoga mats, etc.) but all are completely engaged in their work.

The group of students at the letters and sounds center are putting a giant ABC floor puzzle together. They begin working without a plan, but you can see one start to emerge as they notice how the pieces link together. Students at the word center are practicing friends' names and a few high frequency words. One student has chosen to do a name puzzle. He is laying out his friend's name and checking it against the model. At the reading center, three friends are on their bellies surrounding a book. They are using the illustrations to prompt a retell of the story, *Brown, Bear, Brown, Bear What Do You See?* The listening center is busy with children watching and listening to stories on iPads. They each have their own tablet and are listening to three different stories. Across the room, the writing center is filled with students talking and drawing. As you listen in, the conversation is about the pets they have at home. One student is drawing his cat, Tiger, who loves to hide under his bed.

Meanwhile, the magic is beginning to happen at the small group table for the very first time this year. As Mrs. Jones keeps a careful watch on the rest of the room, she begins her small group lesson. You hear her say, "Okay, let's get started! It's time to become readers!"

Mrs. Jones gets excited each year to begin her small group work with her emergent readers. She knows each child has the potential to become an avid reader and writer and wants to get them started off on the right track. However, she also knows, from experience, that small group work won't be productive if she hasn't laid the groundwork for her students to be independent when working in literacy centers. So, she takes the first six to eight weeks to teach, practice, and reinforce each center's routines and structures that support the development of her readers and writers. She plans for student choice within the five centers. Her goals each year are for students to remain engaged in their literacy centers and be able to solve simple problems on their own; that way, she can focus on teaching her small groups while the other students work independently.

Now, let's explore the learning that happens at the small group table. To teach the emergent reader, you have to understand who the emergent reader is. An emergent reader is simply *someone who is becoming a reader*. That someone could be three years old, five years old, or fifty years old. Age does not matter. *Every* reader starts out on their path to literacy as an emergent reader and their time spent as an emergent reader varies depending on the individual reader and the instruction. In a school setting, our emergent readers are typically in kindergarten or first grade but can certainly be found in older grades too.

Most emergent readers will come to your table:

- Knowing a few letters. (We have had emergent readers who only knew the letters *x* and *o* because they played tic-tac-toe!)
- Developing a concept of what a word is.
- Developing phonemic awareness.
- Developing a sense of story.

With good instruction, most emergent readers will gain control of:

- Left to right directionality.
- One-to-one voice-to-print matching.
- Using known words to begin to monitor their reading.
- Using increasing amounts of meaning, language structure, and visual information (letters and sounds) to monitor their attempts and solve unknown words.

Emergent readers deserve instruction from a skilled teacher who is responsive to their needs in the moment. Skilled teachers have a clear understanding of the emergent reader both academically and emotionally. They know what they need to teach and understand the theory behind their choices as they plan and deliver instruction. They also spend time getting to know the books they are introducing to the small group so their emergent readers can experience success. That success is what makes our readers want to return to our small group table again and again and again!

FUNDAMENTALS FOR TEACHING READING

In his well-known book, *Visible Learning*, John Hattie (2008) presents the results of his meta-analysis of research on factors that influence student learning. Not surprisingly, many factors have effects on learning, including issues from students themselves, the curriculum, and the school. Also not surprising is Hattie's finding that excellence in teaching is the single most powerful influence on achievement. He explains that it's what teachers know, do, and care about that make the difference. This call to action nudges us to continue evolving our understanding of teaching and learning so that we can go from okay results to great results.

With that in mind, let's explore a few of the theoretical understandings that inform our teaching of guided reading. You may be very familiar with some of these ideas and some may be new to you, but keeping these concepts in mind as you work will make a real difference in the moment-by-moment decisions you make in your guided reading lessons. Because they lay the foundation for the why behind our teaching decisions, we'll return to these themes repeatedly throughout this book as we discuss teaching emergent readers at various skill levels.

Reading Is a Complex Process

Have you ever attempted to write your own definition of what it means to read? It's not as easy as it sounds. Literacy theorists define reading in a variety of ways.

- Marie Clay's definition describes reading as a message-getting, problem-solving process (2015).
- Marilyn Adams defines it as a complex process that involves coordinating different skills and systems (1990).
- Louise Rosenblatt's transactional theory explains reading as an interaction between the reader and the print, with the reader's past experiences influencing the meaning making (1978).

Perhaps you've noticed the common thread within these definitions, that reading is much more than learning letters and corresponding sounds. Perhaps in any language, but especially in English, beginning readers progress faster and develop better comprehension skills if they are taught to consider more than just letter sounds as they learn to read. Marie Clay's (2005a, 2005b) important research on emergent readers in their first year of instruction documented what sources of information children used in their attempts at reading. She found patterns in those children who progressed at an average or better rate. Their attempts at reading books showed they attended to various sources of information while making meaning from the print. When analyzing early reading, she found clear examples of at least four types of information. For example, early readers attended to some visual features of the print (such as letters or words), they connected some letters to sounds, they were propelled by their language structure, and they attempted to make meaning.

The complex part for teachers of the earliest readers, however, is helping children begin to attend to all of these at once. The print information is the new and often difficult part for young readers. This can cause one of two pitfalls for teachers. Some teachers tend to focus their instruction almost solely on letters and words, creating inefficient readers. This can actually make the learning of the letters and sounds even harder because the learning is isolated. Other teachers tend to focus so much on meaning and language structure that the texts they provide to their students are completely patterned and easy to memorize, giving young readers a false sense of what reading really is. It takes skill and finesse to create readers who harness these multiple sources of information—rather like a hybrid car that runs on several power sources and uses whatever source is the most efficient at the time. Throughout the rest of this book, we'll be showing you how to teach emergent readers this complex process of using the visual print information, supported by meaning and their language structure.

Learning Is a Physical Change in the Brain

Even after we've been teaching children to read for many years, it still feels almost like magic when a child becomes a fluent reader. Teachers and parents often describe how "it just clicked" for their child or "it all came together." These comments imply a bit of mystery and magic about how this happens. Well, what allows this to happen isn't actually magic. It's a physical change in the brain. The brain becomes "wired" for literacy. And since your job as a teacher is to create the circumstances for this to happen, it's important to keep a bit of brain science in mind as you teach. You don't need to become a neuroscientist but understanding a few general concepts about the brain will help you as a reading teacher.

Neurons That Fire Together Wire Together

When you help a young reader successfully read or write a new word, you are helping their brain cells make connections. You're helping their brains grow in complexity. Pretty exciting stuff!

Carol Lyons (2003) explains how this starts: The brain is composed of neurons, or cells, that are activated through experience. When they "fire," they reach out and can connect with other neurons through their axons. This is the beginning of learning (which, remember, is a change in the brain). If two neurons fire together enough times, they connect, or wire together. This firing and then wiring is the brain's biological procedure for learning. As a simple example, if you want a child to learn the name of the letter *m*, you'll want them to see the letter and say the name at the same time. The name and the visual form will fire and wire together. This starts the physical process of wiring the brain for this knowledge. In this example, think how critical it is that the child is looking at the correct letter, and noticing the details that differentiate an *m* from an *n* or a *w*. Teachers of emergent readers have to pay close attention to where their students are looking because the brain can wire incorrect information just as well as correct.

Practice Makes Permanent

Once the neurons begin firing together, the next important part of this process is practice. If you picture the newly connected neurons of a child who has just started learning the name of the letter *m*, you can imagine a weak connection. We know that new learning is fragile, easily forgotten, and easily confused. We can make these new connections stronger through practice, or the repeated simultaneous firing of neurons. Again, practice isn't magic at all—it's creating a physical change in the brain. Over time, when neurons fire together, they develop faster and stronger connections between the neurons, which makes for more automatic responses by the learner. Fluency and automaticity are physically wired in the brain.

This is why a child who has had tons of experience in naming and using the letter *m* will know it automatically and not forget it. This is just as true for the child who has been calling a *d* a *b* for two years or the child who consistently looks at the last letter of a word first. They've practiced the wrong things. Teachers, however, can use this brain knowledge to undo incorrect responding or even prevent it from happening in the first place.

Teach the Whole Brain

The next bit of advice that we get from neuroscience involves teaching so the learner's whole brain becomes activated. In *The Art of Changing the Brain*, James Zull (2002) explains that the "back brain" takes in information, or perceptions, from the senses and the "front brain" uses those perceptions to problem solve, make decisions, and make meaning. Readers go back and forth between taking in information and using the information to make meaning.

The back brain includes the occipital lobe for sight, the temporal lobe for sound, and the parietal lobe for movement. You're probably already aware of the idea of multisensory teaching. When learning *items* (letters or words), activating auditory, visual, and kinesthetic senses can result in faster, more complete learning. Reminding ourselves that children need to *see it, say it, and move it* can help us make sure we are activating the sensory lobes. Think about the difference between learning words through flashcards and learning words through writing or building with magnetic letters.

The front brain includes the frontal lobe for using information to make decisions, make meaning, problem solve, look for patterns, and correct error. You're probably also aware of the importance of reading instruction that is focused on the process of making meaning. Most reading teachers would associate these skills with comprehension instruction.

Here's the rub—too often our teaching focuses on either the back brain or the front brain. We are either teaching skills (such as phonics or phonemic awareness or spelling) or we are teaching comprehension (thinking about what is read). Some theories of reading erroneously go as far as promoting that we teach "skills" (back brain) from k-2, before teaching comprehension (front brain) from third grade on. Zull is emphatic that teachers will get better results if they design instruction meant to activate both the front and the back brain from the start. In other words, our instruction should invite children to learn skills in the meaningful context of whole text reading and writing. Since our youngest readers have so much to learn, it can be tempting to devote most of our lesson time to teaching *items* and not enough time to teaching how to problem solve with those items. An approach based in best practices, then, would dictate the need to activate the front and back brain by using multisensory approaches to teaching skills, but dedicating most of our time to using these skills in real reading and writing contexts. Our children need to read books and write stories as they learn skills.

Emotion Is the Gatekeeper

What emotional reactions have you seen from children in your classroom when it's time for them to read or write? Hopefully, most children feel joy and excitement, but you've probably also seen children exhibit anger, avoidance, or tears. Emotions are connected to all learning experiences, both good and bad. Emotion can motivate us to stick with a challenge or can deflate us to the point of giving up. When you're learning something that you care about and are experiencing success, you feel great and want to keep at it. On the other hand, when you are faced with a challenge that you have no interest in or one that feels too difficult, it's hard to stay engaged.

How can we help all children associate literacy with positive emotions? And why is it so critically important that they do? Again, it's important to think about what's physically happening in the brain during learning experiences (Lyons 2003).

- When we have positive experiences, such as success in learning or solving a hard problem, the brain releases *dopamine*. This chemical makes us feel good, increases motivation, and aids in memory. We engage more in the positive experience. We want to take on the challenge. It's easy to see why we want our young readers' brains to release as much of this as possible! The more children associate positive feelings with reading, the more they will read!
- When we have negative experiences, such as trying a task that's too hard, the brain releases *cortisol*. Cortisol is a stress hormone and it interferes with learning and memory. So once things go south in a learning situation, cortisol makes any further learning unlikely. It becomes hard to remember and hard to try.
- When we feel particularly threatened in a learning situation, chemicals launch the "fight or flight" reaction. Our brain tells us to either rebel against the threat or get out of Dodge. These reactions can look like misbehavior in our students.
- The reticular activating system is a small structure in the brain that acts as a gatekeeper, helping to control attention. When this system is activated, stressful stimuli are blocked out, stopping the ability to attend. The brain is protecting the learner from the unpleasant threat. Once that gate is closed, learning is going to stop.

Because of these physical reactions in the brain, success breeds more success and failure, unfortunately, breeds more failure. We have to be especially aware of this with our earliest readers. We are helping to set the stage for their future feelings about literacy. The good news is that guided reading by its very nature gives emergent readers a perfect platform for loving to read and write. Why? Well-planned guided reading lessons pitch the learning at the students' cutting edge of learning, with enough independent work for them to feel in control and enough challenge for them to feel motivated to tackle new learning. Teachers of guided reading become experts in selecting new books that feel like a perfect fit for their students. Teachers learn to provide scaffolds for new skills until students are ready to try on their own. Teachers incorporate some choice for students in their familiar reading, as a way to build agency and engagement. All these instructional strategies prime the young brain for positive feelings about reading and writing.

GUIDED READING: FROM FUNDAMENTALS TO PRACTICE

Guided reading (Fountas and Pinnell 1996, Pinnell and Fountas 2017, Richardson 2016) is the perfect format for teaching from the theoretical positions we've just described. The small group format allows for differentiating instruction efficiently for an entire classroom. Guided reading is also a bit of a paradox. On one hand, it is very structured, with defined components. On the other hand, it's an extremely flexible vessel that requires you to decide what instruction is needed for particular children on a particular day. We'll look now at the structure of guided reading and see what components define an effective guided reading lesson, along with some guiding principles to make them successful. Later, we'll explore how you can continually adapt these components according to the changing needs of the children at your table.

Reading Books

Reading books occurs in every lesson and your first important job is book selection. For emergent readers you'll consider factors such as book level (pre-A through D), which words are used, how the text is laid out, the sentence structure, and the interest level, just to name a few. Then, when it's time to read, you will have three important tasks: introducing the book to the group, supporting them as they read it, and leading a quick discussion afterward.

Introducing the Book Before Reading

The purpose of introducing a book to children is to provide a scaffold that allows them to read the book that's a bit out of their reach, independently. We select books that are a slight stretch for our students, giving them the opportunity to grow. Then we scaffold their reading by providing a supportive book introduction, being cautious not to give away everything about the book by overintroducing it.

A good book introduction:

- Should be short so that we allow plenty of time for the reading of the book and the discussion afterward.
- Will get children excited to read. They should feel they have a purpose for jumping right into the book.
- Offers some glimpses into the plot or text structure, so the children understand the big idea of the story.
- Helps children hear or rehearse any tricky language structures they might encounter in the book by using that same language as you introduce the book. Book language often sounds different from students' daily oral language, so allowing them to hear a different structure beforehand will make the text more accessible.
- Allows children to look at a bit of print. You'll choose a few valuable words or phrases for them to examine. This will make that print easier to handle when they encounter it while reading the book.

Scaffolding During the Reading

- You will usually have your students read individually in guided reading. Occasionally, you may choose to use choral reading or partner reading and we'll explain those techniques in later chapters. Avoid round robin reading, where children take turns reading the text out loud. This practice is not effective for many reasons. The most important reason is that it drastically reduces the amount of reading each student gets to practice. For individual oral reading to work with a small group, you need to establish some clear routines so that children aren't disrupting each other.
- Children *whisper read* orally in these early levels and you will listen in to each student, coaching as needed. Oral reading at this stage allows you to check on early reading behaviors and provide help. In your first guided reading lessons, you'll want to model what *whisper reading* sounds like and allow students to practice reading at a volume that is loud enough for you to hear, but not loud enough to disturb the other students.
- Some teachers choose to *stagger-start* their students, so they don't begin choral reading the same page at the same time. You may want to pass out the books one by one slowly, starting them at different times. You could also hand out books to every other student first to allow different start times. Eventually, with longer, more complex books, you won't need to do this, but in the early levels it's easy for students to begin choral reading and losing their own concentration.

- Plan for readers to finish their books at different rates. Teach them a routine for what to do when they finish if others are still reading. Perhaps you'll have them read the book again or look for their favorite pages to re-read with a partner from the group.
- Your most important role will be to teach and support your readers in the heat of the moment, as they process text. This is the beauty of guided reading—being right there when the rubber meets the road. The coming chapters will guide you in what to look for and what to teach as your students read emergent-level books.

Discussing and Teaching After the Reading

- The first thing you say to children after they read a book tells them what you value, so make sure the first talk after they finish the book is about what they think. Have a natural conversation about the story, just as a parent would with a child after a bedtime story. What did they think of the story? Did something make them laugh, surprise them, intrigue them? Did it remind them of anything? Talk about it!
- After a brief conversation, you'll choose one or maybe two teaching points you want the whole group to learn. You'll have an idea what it might be based on the level of text, but you won't decide this until you've observed them reading during this lesson. You'll teach in response to what they show you they need.

Writing

We believe that reading and writing are reciprocal. Each teaches the same process but from a different angle. If you want your children to become good readers, teach them through writing. Think about the most common reading behaviors that your children demonstrate before they become proficient. They most likely don't look at the print. They make up the story. They ignore letters or words that they don't know. And they "read" very quickly, with their speech going much faster than their eyes can scan the print. Think about this: it's very possible to *read* a word without ever noticing all the letters. Some children recognize some words just based on a few salient letters or how the word looks in general. This is why nonreaders can read words like *McDonalds* without knowing all the letters in the words. In writing, however, you *have* to look at every single letter as you write it. You must notice the details. Reading builds up language quickly, while writing breaks down language slowly.

Writing within guided reading looks a little different from other classroom writing, like writer's workshop or journal writing. In guided reading, you are designing opportunities for your students to learn the skills they need in reading. For this reason, we dictate the sentences the group will write during early levels. Just as leveled text gives children just the right amount of print with carefully selected language, we try to carefully craft sentences that do the same thing. We'll give you suggestions for the types of sentences you can craft and help you choose what to teach. In general, you'll create opportunities for your children to learn how print works, how to learn useful words, how to learn letters and sounds, and how to hear and transcribe the sounds they hear in words.

Both you and your students will be writing, so you need a plan for materials. Figure 1.1 shows what we suggest.

Materials	How and Why?
Large chart paper, white board, or tabletop chart paper	■ Teacher models the writing, in large clear print. ■ The closer the print is to the students, the better.
Student writing book	■ Turn the writing book so it opens bottom to top. ■ Students use the bottom page for their story and the top page for practicing new learning.
Markers (dark colored)	■ Dark, bold print pops off the page and aids in their learning to look at print.
Correction tape	■ Quickly covers up mistakes ■ Avoids the mess of erasing
Yellow highlighter markers	■ For drawing boxes to scaffold hearing sounds in words
Scissors	■ For cutting up sentences

FIGURE 1.1

Materials for Small Group Reading

Learning Letters and Words

Every lesson for emergent readers will include opportunities to learn letters, letter sounds, and high frequency words. The goal is to be able to use letters and high frequency words with automaticity, or very little conscious attention, freeing up brain power for other kinds of thinking. We'll have suggestions for what letters and words to teach and how as you move through the levels, but some general principles apply for all memory-type learning.

- Remember to engage as many lobes of the brain as you can. Children learn fastest if they use their eyes, ears, mouth, and body. Children need to voice what they are learning as they are looking at it. We'll show you how to use tracing, writing, and moving magnetic letters as a kinesthetic component to learning. Remember that if you have children *see it, say it, move it* they'll be engaging many lobes of their brain.
- Expose students to their new learning across space and across time. This means that the same new letters and words should pop up across all the components of your lessons, and then pop up again across days and weeks. Repeated exposure and practice over time will result in the automaticity they need.
- Context helps our brains have a hook for new learning. Choose the letters and words you teach by pulling them out of books or writing. Let students visualize where they needed to use the letters or words. Then once you've taught something in isolation, go back to the book or writing and explore how that item works in context. Otherwise, the learning seems random and will be easily forgotten.

Learning How Words Work

Emergent readers are just beginning to understand the hierarchical nature of language. Sounds combine to make words, words combine to make sentences, and sentences combine to make stories. This learning is huge and foundational. The early levels are our playground for exploring these concepts. One common problem that we've seen is teachers asking children to "sound out" words when the children don't yet understand the nature of sequential sounds matching sequential letters on the page. We need to make this very explicit to children in both reading and writing. Again, engaging various lobes of the brain makes the learning easier. We will show you how to use magnetic letters, writing with sound boxes, and masking cards to teach this concept.

These components represent the structure of guided reading lessons and give you a framework within which to make great teaching decisions. The rest of this book will guide you in how to make those great decisions as you use a gradient of leveled books with your emergent readers. We remember when we were novices and a mentor told us, "If you do nothing but these components, you'll be helping kids. But if you learn to make really smart choices within the components, you'll see your kids take off." So, now we are saying that to you.

WHAT IS HAPPENING DURING LITERACY CENTERS?

At this point, you may be asking yourself the million-dollar question: What are the rest of the students doing in their literacy centers while you're teaching your small groups? This is a big question and the answer isn't simple. What works for one group of students may not work for another. Sometimes you have to go through a bit of trial and error, rethink, and try something new. So, though we can offer suggestions, you are the only person who can make decisions for your group of students.

However, you might take an important piece of advice from successful teachers by not beginning small group reading until after the first six to eight weeks of school are under your belt. Instead, spend that valuable time setting up your literacy centers and teaching your students to be independent in them. There will be plenty of teaching, reteaching, reinforcing, redirecting, and reminding. But trust us, taking the time upfront to teach for independence during literacy centers will be worth it in the end! Work with your students until they understand:

- Explicitly how to do the activities in each center.
- How to figure out which center to go to.
- Where to locate materials.
- How to use the materials and the different possibilities for doing so.
- Where students are permitted to work, especially if you have a flexible seating classroom.
- What to do if they think they are finished but time isn't up.
- How to solve any problems that come up.
- How to get help if they need it.
- How to clean up when literacy centers are over.

We have created an online resource you can refer to for ideas for your literacy centers that support the learning taking place at the small group table. See www.stenhouse.com/content /intentional-from-the-start.

Remember You're the Expert at the Small Group Table

If you haven't patted yourself on the back recently for being a professional educator, do it right now. Take a moment to acknowledge that your job as a teacher of young children requires an enormous amount of know-how. You have to know how young brains learn. You have to know how literacy develops. You have to know how to use the best instructional techniques. That's a lot of know-how, but even that's not enough. Every child that sits at your small group table has a different repertoire of literacy skills. They come to you with different experiences, different strengths, and different habits. You need to know each of them as individual readers. What can each child do on their own? What do they try when they don't know a word? What can they do with a little help? What areas need to be strengthened? Notice in Figure 1.2 where the expert teacher's areas of knowledge intersect. We love guided reading because this format honors each area of the teacher's knowledge.

In our next chapters, we'll be looking more closely at the details of supporting readers as they progress in skills through the earliest levels of text. We'll look at how each instructional procedure is adapted when students reach a new level of independence with harder books. The differences between a Level B book and a Level C book may not be readily apparent, but the differences are important and purposeful. We'll help you see the genius of these carefully crafted texts and become better at using their fine gradient of difficulty to support your readers. You'll be coaxing your readers into slightly deeper water and showing them how to stay afloat with less and less support. The best part will be the joy and confidence your students will feel, as they become stronger and stronger readers, enjoying the many wonderful stories they'll encounter along the way.

CHAPTER 1

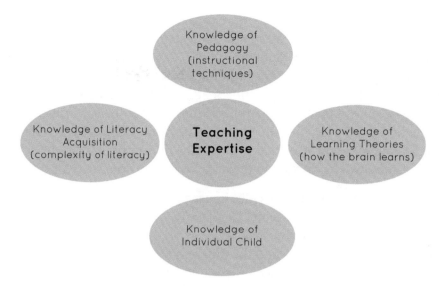

FIGURE 1.2

Areas of Teacher Expertise

Choosing Books Children Are Ready to Read

The books you teach with, as much as your readers' skills, determine the success of their reading. Think about it like a swimming lesson. When swimmers jump into the pool, hopefully their instructor will have made a wise choice for this. Do they need a baby pool? The shallow end? Deep end? The ocean? You'll make similar decisions in guided reading. How much challenge will best support your young reader? What types of words, sentences, stories, and pictures will help keep them afloat?

To make the perfect instructional match, teachers need an expert understanding of three things: literacy acquisition theory, the children in their classroom, and the books on their shelves. These three factors work together to create the magic that's possible at the guided reading table. In short, we'll never make expert decisions about instructional books unless we know what our children know how to do on their own, what they need to know next, and what books could provide that opportunity. The next questions become, "How do we make effective efficient instructional book choices? Are leveled libraries the way to go?"

THE ROLE OF LEVELED BOOKS IN EMERGENT LITERACY

If you follow the ever-swinging pendulum of which teaching practices are lauded and which are maligned in the education world, you'll know the use of leveled books is currently taking some heat. We think that perhaps, like most good ideas in education, the use of leveled texts has, in some cases, been taken too far. Educators are rightly questioning if it's harmful to restrict readers to books at their "just right" level. Are we decreasing engagement? Are we shaming children? Are we holding them back?

Let's take a step back to review why, for whom, and how books were originally leveled, in an effort to reflect on the value of this practice.

Who Needs Leveled Books and Why Do They Need Them?

In the United States, Reading Recovery®, an early literacy intervention, is probably responsible for the first taste of leveled books as we know them today. This intervention is based on the idea that children can be scaffolded in learning to read by using a fine gradient of increasingly complex text. When Reading Recovery® came to the United States in the 1980s, the leveled books used seemed different from the basal stories that were predominant at the time. The little leveled books used natural language patterns and were not designed around a single phonics pattern. They were designed to encourage children to use meaning, their existing knowledge of language structure, and various phonics skills as they read. Leveled books allowed children to read books in whatever sequence and pace worked for them, unlike the basal readers. The gradient in difficulty between levels was so fine that a layman might not even be able to notice the difference between two levels. This was purposeful. For the earliest readers who are just beginning to navigate print, each shaky step forward must be small.

If we believe in Vygotsky and Cole's ideas about scaffolding and the zone of proximal development being the sweet spot for instruction (Vygotsky and Cole 1981), a gradient of leveled books is very helpful. For the earliest readers, print can seem like a sea of confusing black marks. If our objective for early readers is to keep their eyes on print, scanning left to right, it's helpful to have just the right amount of familiar print on the page to anchor their looking. This is what leveled text provides—just the right amount of familiar and just the right amount of new. The leveling system provides teachers with a tool to help them match children with books that would scaffold their reading.

So where does the controversy come in? We became level crazy. Since little leveled readers were so popular and worked so well for emergent readers in kindergarten and first grade, teachers and publishers expanded their use to second grade. And third. And fourth. And on up. Programs like Accelerated Reader® became popular in guiding students to "just right" Lexile levels, even up through middle school. Teachers began basing grades on levels. Levels morphed from a teacher's tool for selecting books that emergent readers could access, to a fence that kept students who could already read from accessing books they might enjoy. By the time readers are past the early stages of reading, they should have developed the skills to self-select books and monitor their own reading. At this stage, over-reliance on levels to guide reading can certainly be problematic.

A second problem that has emerged is the identity crisis that students are facing by being told their level and being referred to as a particular level. As a result, some students' reading identities aren't considered based on what they love to read or why they love to read. They are based on what level they read. And with that level comes a judgment. "I'm a high reader." "I'm a normal reader." "I'm a bad reader and I'm ashamed." It seems the culture of instruction took a good idea and expanded it into a problem.

How Can We Use Leveled Books Well?

Before we throw the baby out with the bathwater, let's think about how we can use leveled books to our children's advantage in early primary classrooms.

1. Don't tell children "their level." Children *read* levels—they don't *become* those levels. Our innocent young children won't worry about levels if we don't advertise them. Let's take this source of anxiety off their plates.

2. Think of book levels in "bands" of levels. Leveling is an imprecise science. All Level C books, for example, will not be of equal difficulty to all children who "test" at Level C. So, most children who benchmark at Level D will find some appropriate books at Levels C and E.

3. Make sure there is time in every day for children to have completely free exploration of books of all levels and topics. Whether you call this time "independent reading" or some other label, we want to be clear that children should have lots of time to read on their own outside of their small group time with you.

In our years in education, we've seen many good ideas take a wrong turn. This usually happens because the idea gets overgeneralized and overused. Or perhaps the rationale behind the original idea isn't understood fully and just becomes something we do on autopilot. Our stance on leveled books is the same as our stance on everything we do as teachers—we need to understand the *why* of what we do before we can ever do the *how* effectively. We think leveled books are critical in the early primary classroom, when they are used as a scaffolding tool and not as a label.

HOW LEVELS ARE DETERMINED

The world of leveled books is murky water for many teachers, administrators, and parents. One reason is the variety of book-leveling systems. Books can be leveled with a level number (DRA 10), or a level letter (Fountas & Pinnell H), or a Lexile number (420), or a basal level (pre-primer.) Some book publishers of beginning reader trade books label their books with level numbers that relate in no way to any of the above leveling systems. Some systems use only quantitative measures such as vocabulary and sentence length. Other systems also take into account story complexity or maturity of theme. It's easy to see why levels are a source of confusion.

For our purposes, let's explore a bit about what a level can mean and what it might look like in the early levels. Although there are variations, in general we can trust most publishers of the little readers typically used in classrooms to have considered some common factors, such as:

- interest level for the age group
- plot complexity
- picture support
- text layout
- predictability
- repetition or variation of sentence structures
- sentence length and complexity
- word count
- word choice (high frequency words, vocabulary, decodable words)

When writing leveled books for the popular PM readers, Beverly Randell (1999) considered all these factors and more. She also considered which words were used frequently in children's own writing and oral language, which words would add interest for children, and at which point to begin using past tense versus present tense. The variety of factors considered gives a fair bit of dependability to levels. Not complete dependability, just fair dependability. This dependability helps make a level a great starting point for selecting a book for a lesson.

Variations in Difficulty Within Levels

If you examine all the books you have within a certain level, you're going to find that some books seem harder than others. They are. And that's actually a good thing. If we want to be responsive to our children, we need book choices that give them exposure to a variety of challenges as they progress through the levels. We want to create flexible readers, so we need flexible choices. Take a look at some text examples from Levels A, B, C, and D in Figures 2.1 to 2.4. What variations in difficulty do you see within each level? Do you notice levels overlapping each other in difficulty?

Here are two Level A books (Figure 2.1) from the Handprints collection. Let's analyze each book's difficulty in terms of meaning, language structure, and print information.

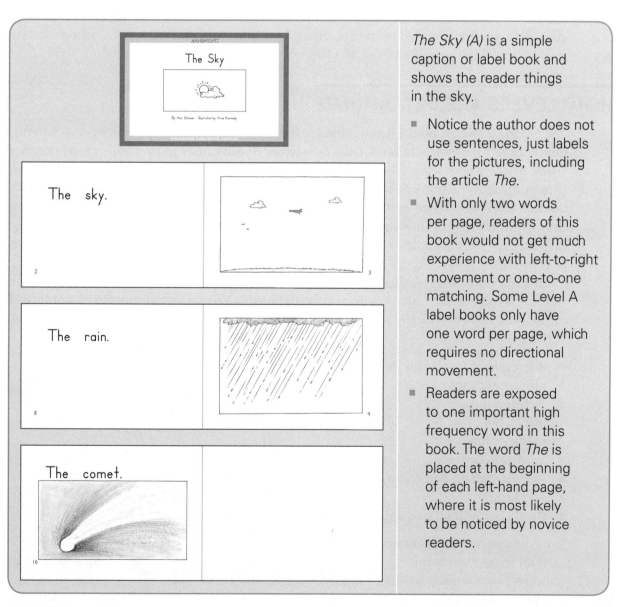

The Sky (A) is a simple caption or label book and shows the reader things in the sky.

- Notice the author does not use sentences, just labels for the pictures, including the article *The*.

- With only two words per page, readers of this book would not get much experience with left-to-right movement or one-to-one matching. Some Level A label books only have one word per page, which requires no directional movement.

- Readers are exposed to one important high frequency word in this book. The word *The* is placed at the beginning of each left-hand page, where it is most likely to be noticed by novice readers.

FIGURE 2.1
Level A Book Comparison

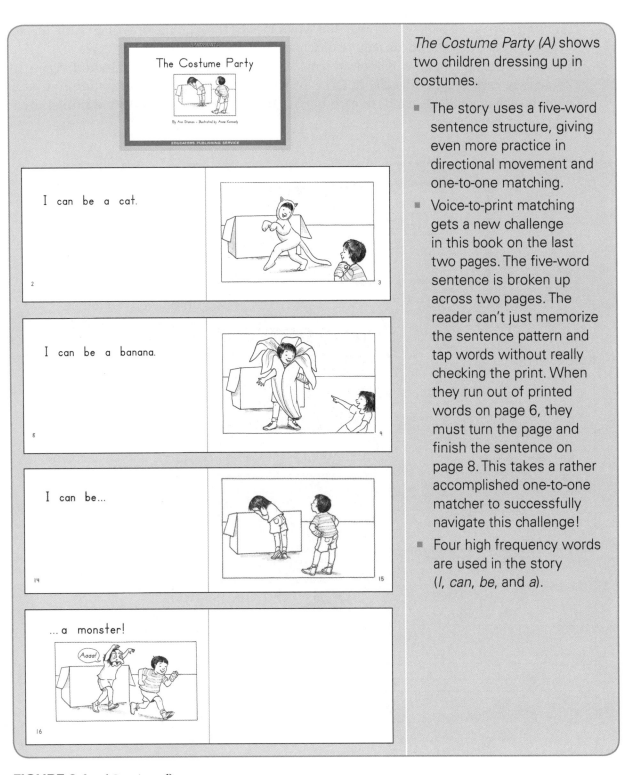

The Costume Party (A) shows two children dressing up in costumes.

- The story uses a five-word sentence structure, giving even more practice in directional movement and one-to-one matching.

- Voice-to-print matching gets a new challenge in this book on the last two pages. The five-word sentence is broken up across two pages. The reader can't just memorize the sentence pattern and tap words without really checking the print. When they run out of printed words on page 6, they must turn the page and finish the sentence on page 8. This takes a rather accomplished one-to-one matcher to successfully navigate this challenge!

- Four high frequency words are used in the story (*I*, *can*, *be*, and *a*).

FIGURE 2.1 (*Continued*)

At first glance, they look very similar, but when viewed through the eyes of an early literacy teacher, we see that the books require different skills even within the same level.

Now, here are two Level B books (Figure 2.2) from the Handprints collection. Again, try to analyze each book's difficulty in terms of meaning, language structure, and print information. What are the demands of each book? Does the "easier" Level B seem similar to the "harder" Level A?

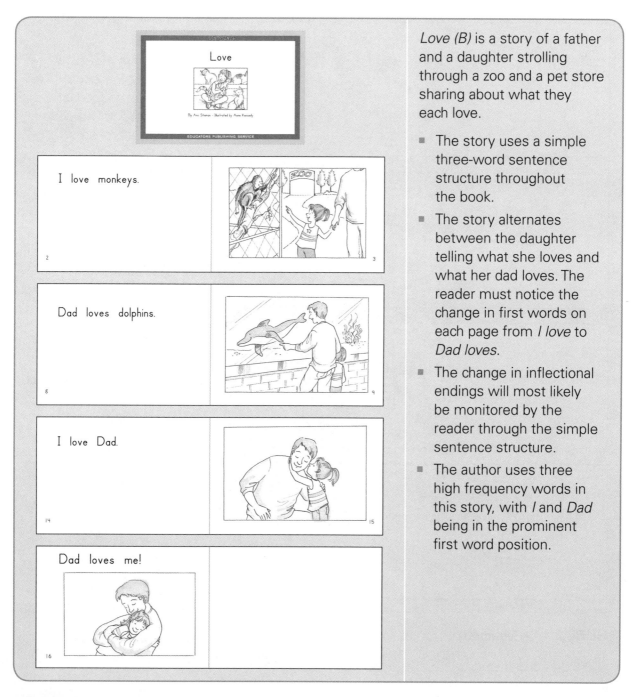

Love (B) is a story of a father and a daughter strolling through a zoo and a pet store sharing about what they each love.

- The story uses a simple three-word sentence structure throughout the book.

- The story alternates between the daughter telling what she loves and what her dad loves. The reader must notice the change in first words on each page from *I love* to *Dad loves*.

- The change in inflectional endings will most likely be monitored by the reader through the simple sentence structure.

- The author uses three high frequency words in this story, with *I* and *Dad* being in the prominent first word position.

FIGURE 2.2
Level B Book Comparison

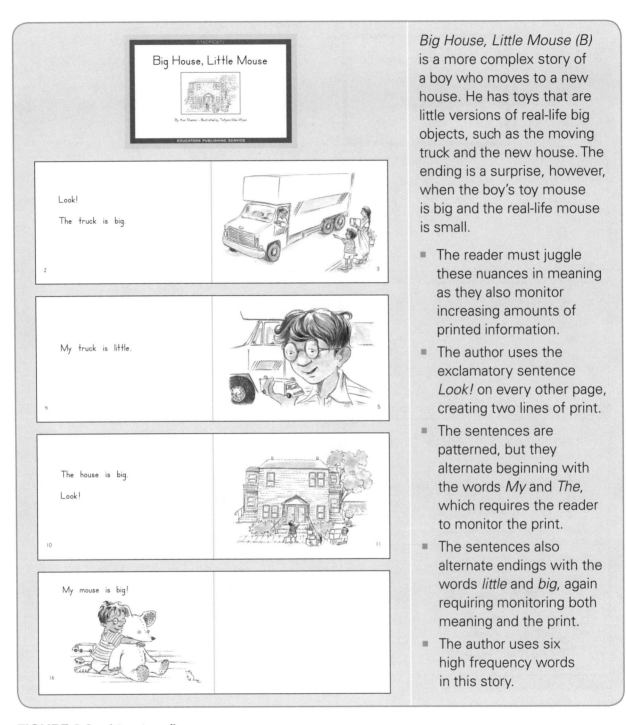

Big House, Little Mouse (B) is a more complex story of a boy who moves to a new house. He has toys that are little versions of real-life big objects, such as the moving truck and the new house. The ending is a surprise, however, when the boy's toy mouse is big and the real-life mouse is small.

- The reader must juggle these nuances in meaning as they also monitor increasing amounts of printed information.
- The author uses the exclamatory sentence *Look!* on every other page, creating two lines of print.
- The sentences are patterned, but they alternate beginning with the words *My* and *The*, which requires the reader to monitor the print.
- The sentences also alternate endings with the words *little* and *big*, again requiring monitoring both meaning and the print.
- The author uses six high frequency words in this story.

CHAPTER 2

FIGURE 2.2   (*Continued*)

Here are two Level C books (Figure 2.3) from the Handprints collection. Notice the steep jump in difficulty within this level. As we will explore later in this book, readers at this stage have so much new information to pull together that we really need a wide variety of books to support them. Do you think our first example of a Level C book is more similar to the Level B books or more like the hardest Level C book?

CHAPTER 2

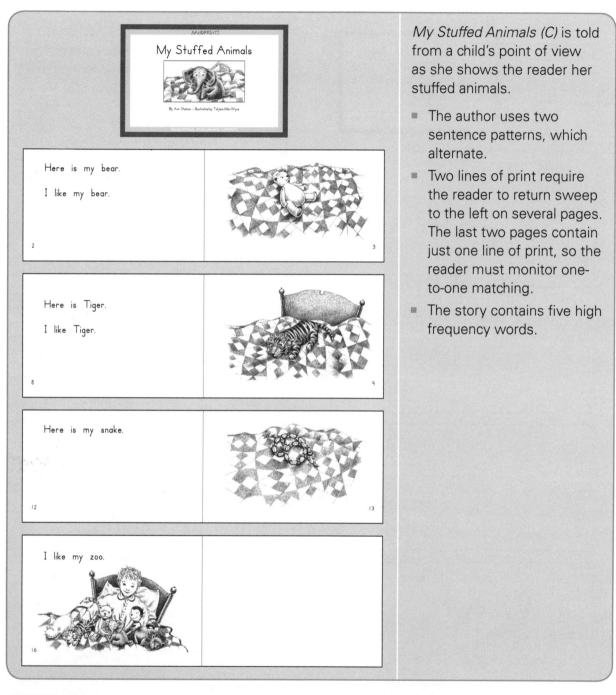

My Stuffed Animals (C) is told from a child's point of view as she shows the reader her stuffed animals.

- The author uses two sentence patterns, which alternate.
- Two lines of print require the reader to return sweep to the left on several pages. The last two pages contain just one line of print, so the reader must monitor one-to-one matching.
- The story contains five high frequency words.

FIGURE 2.3
Level C Book Comparison

A Hot Day (C) is a story about two children playing outside and negotiating whether they play together or not.

- The print volume increases with up to sixteen words per page and four lines of print.
- The reader is introduced to words with inflectional endings such as *-ed* and *-ing* that need to be monitored with both sentence structure and printed visual information.
- The story uses thirteen high frequency words and words that may need some simple decoding.

FIGURE 2.3 (*Continued*)

Finally, let's take a look at two Level D books (Figure 2.4) from the Handprints collection. Once students begin reading Level D texts, they must have both one-to-one voice print matching under control and left-to-right directionality across several lines of text. They also need to have built a bank of high frequency words that will help them to monitor their reading. Level D texts have *more* lines of text, *more* variation in sentence lengths, *more* high frequency words, *more* dialogue, and *more* words to solve using meaning, language structure,

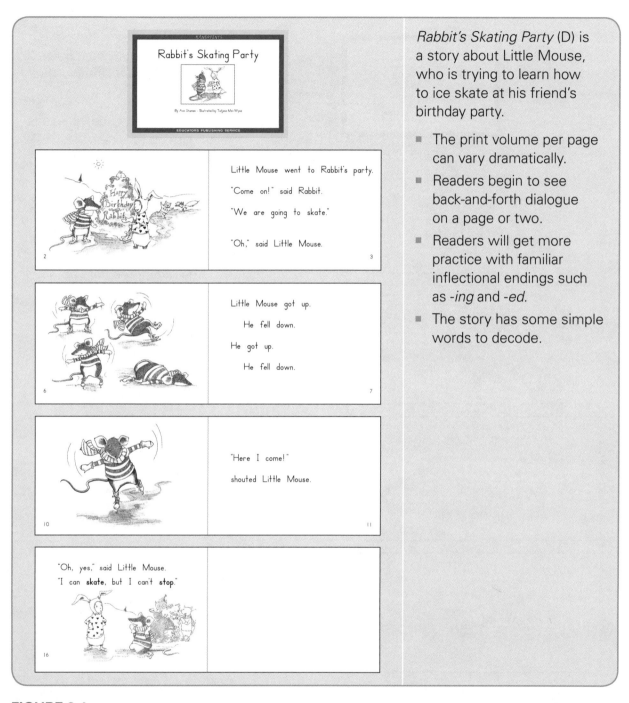

Rabbit's Skating Party

Little Mouse went to Rabbit's party.

"Come on!" said Rabbit.

"We are going to skate."

"Oh," said Little Mouse.

Little Mouse got up.

He fell down.

He got up.

He fell down.

"Here I come!"

shouted Little Mouse.

"Oh, yes," said Little Mouse.

"I can **skate**, but I can't **stop**."

Rabbit's Skating Party (D) is a story about Little Mouse, who is trying to learn how to ice skate at his friend's birthday party.

- The print volume per page can vary dramatically.
- Readers begin to see back-and-forth dialogue on a page or two.
- Readers will get more practice with familiar inflectional endings such as -*ing* and -*ed*.
- The story has some simple words to decode.

FIGURE 2.4

Level D Book Comparison

and visual information (letters and sounds). Think about this: How do Levels A, B, and C set readers up for success in Level D?

Like everything about literacy, book levels are complex, with varying levels of challenge. One book may have challenging vocabulary but more simple sentence structures. Another book might have varied sentence structures but rely heavily on repeated high frequency words.

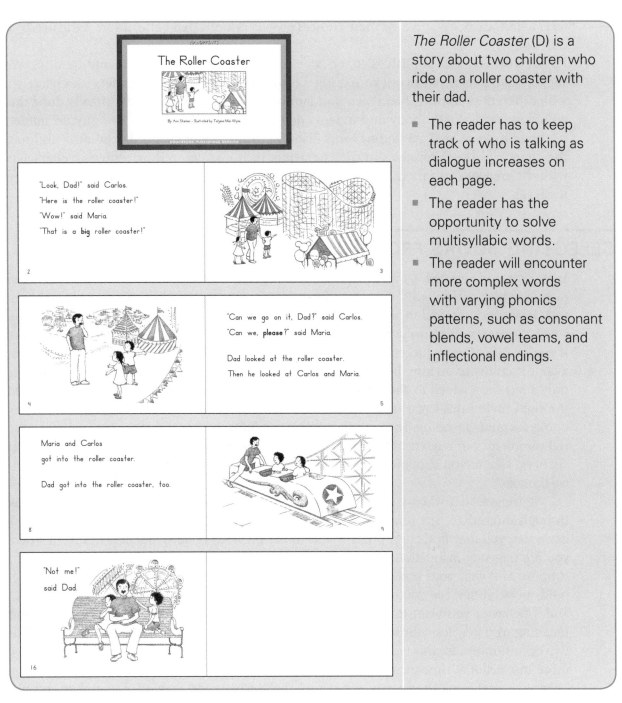

The Roller Coaster (D) is a story about two children who ride on a roller coaster with their dad.

- The reader has to keep track of who is talking as dialogue increases on each page.
- The reader has the opportunity to solve multisyllabic words.
- The reader will encounter more complex words with varying phonics patterns, such as consonant blends, vowel teams, and inflectional endings.

CHAPTER 2

FIGURE 2.4   (*Continued*)

These variations can increase the difficulty for one child, while reducing it for another. You probably also noticed that levels can overlap, even within one publisher's collection. Your book baskets probably contain more than one publisher, so your levels will overlap even more. And we're actually glad about this. Going on autopilot through text levels removes two of the factors we talked about previously—our knowledge of our children and our knowledge of literacy acquisition. We appreciate and seek out publishers that provide a range of texts within each level because these choices give us options that better address the needs of our groups.

We also seek out publishers that offer books with diverse characters and families. We suggest taking an inventory of your guided reading library. Will your readers see characters with different skin tones, hair types, and family members? You may have already done this with your read aloud library and independent reading library but check out your guided reading library as well. As Rudine Sims Bishop (1990) taught us, books can offer children the chance to see themselves in the characters in books, as well as centering characters with differences from them. Both are critical. Book choice is about so much more than the level!

SELECTING BOOKS FROM LEVEL BANDS

Have you ever selected a watermelon from the grocery store? Do you have a method for picking which melon will be the best for your picnic? Some melon choosers do a thump test. How does the melon sound when you thump it? Some use the smell test. Can you smell the melon fragrance when you sniff it? Some use a color test. Some use a shape test. If you're a super savvy picker, you'll consider all those factors. You'll also hope the store has a large quantity of melons, because your chances of getting a good one decrease if there are only a few from which to choose. Of course, you won't actually know for sure if you picked the right melon until you cut it open and try it. The same might be said about selecting books for guided reading. The more factors we consider, the better our chance of picking the right book for our readers. If we only consider the publisher's stated level, we decrease our chances. Like melon shopping, the more titles we have as possibilities, the better matches we'll make.

We suggest that when you "shop" for books in your guided reading baskets, you look through more than one level. Give yourself more choices. As we saw in the earlier book examples, you may find appropriate books in the previous or subsequent levels from where you are targeting instruction. If you identify the major reading behaviors you're hoping to support, and view your book choices through that lens, you may find more than one level holds possibilities. For example, let's say that your group has begun reading Level D books and a behavior you want to develop is solving short words using visual information and meaning. You may look through your Level C books to find a book that includes just one or two opportunities for this type of solving. Since the rest of the book may be easy, you'll have more instructional time to really model how to solve a word while maintaining meaning. Then your next book choice may come from the D basket and may offer several opportunities to solve words of this nature. Because you modeled it in easier text, your readers got to practice in the "shallow end" before trying it in deeper water. Many teachers also have unofficial benchmark books at each level that they use to determine if it's time to bump up and shop in the next band of levels. Once you know your books really well, and have used them with many children, you'll find that some books in a level seem very easy. These books are good entry books into a level. Other books seem to present challenges to most groups until they are very strong at that level. These books can be good exit books, signaling readiness to move up.

REMEMBER THE PURPOSE OF TEACHING WITH LEVELED BOOKS

It's easy in literacy instruction to lose sight of the big picture and get caught up in checklists of behaviors and known items. Checklists for levels can be valuable and we've certainly used them to help us think about our children. But remember the purpose of leveling books is not to check off items or behaviors. The purpose is to scaffold learning opportunities. As the teaching expert, your job is to identify what your children need to learn to do and then find the best books to give them the chance to learn those behaviors. Book levels are just a tool to help you narrow down your search. Be flexible as you choose books. Change your language from "I need a Level B book," to "I need a book that will allow my readers to check their meaningful attempts at unknown words with the first sound." You are the swim coach here, and you decide how deep the water needs to be. In the next chapters, we'll dive into these bands of levels and explore what teaching and learning can look like once we've found the right water for our new swimmers.

Learning Where to Look

As Mrs. Jones prepares for her small group work for the week, she starts by analyzing her letter identification assessments to see who is learning letters fast and who is struggling with letter learning. She notices that thirteen of her students know forty or more upper- and lowercase letters. Three students know between thirty and forty letters and two students know fewer than thirteen letters. This data is promising, but there are some students who need some targeted letter work to accelerate their letter learning.

   Mrs. Jones peruses her students' *My Writing* books. She looks for students who are only illustrating stories and students who are illustrating and attempting to write. Of those students taking the risk to begin to write, she notes who is:

➤ randomly placing words on a page.

➤ attempting to use kid spelling by labeling their pictures.

➤ using the high frequency words that have been introduced and spelling them correctly.

➤ attempting to write sentences using a mix of high frequency words and kid spelling.

➤ using correct left to right directionality.

➤ putting spaces between their words.

➤ using a period as their punctuation mark.

Gathering this information from her students' writing will guide her in designing the instruction that needs to take place when they engage with books and writing at the small group table.

From conferring with students during Writer's Workshop, Mrs. Jones decided to assess letter sounds in isolation for the first time this month because many of her students are already attempting to use kid spelling. Surprisingly, nine of her students can produce twenty or more sounds. Six students can produce fifteen to nineteen sounds and three students produce fewer than fourteen letter sounds. She now knows who needs to do some targeted sound sorts during the *letter learning* portion of her small group reading lesson, as well as who is ready to use sound boxes during the writing portion of the lesson.

Mrs. Jones decides to divide her class into four small groups this week. She will have a group using teacher-created Pre-A texts to focus on learning letters and where to look at print. She will have two groups that will focus on how to look at print and learning new high frequency words using Level A texts. The last group will focus on learning to look closer at print and using what they already know while reading Level B texts.

Assessments and analyzing data are very important *if* they inform teachers about their next instructional moves. Like Mrs. Jones, we must be very intentional about what we choose to assess, how we assess, and when we assess. As you observe your own students in action and analyze data, ask yourself these two critical questions:

- What does the child know and control?
- What is the child ready to learn?

Exploring these questions can help you plan focused small group lessons based on each child's zone of proximal development (Vygotsky and Cole 1981). Because students develop as readers at different rates, your small groups will be fluid, with children moving in and out based on need and instructional goals. Fortunately, a "bluebird" is no longer a "bluebird" all year long!

If you teach in the early elementary grades, you have probably had children in your class who are not ready for a Level A text and had to plan for their learning. As you think about our two questions, consider the varied characteristics of children who need their first formal exposure to text to be at the Pre-A level (see Figure 3.1).

CHILDREN WHO DON'T LOOK AT PRINT YET

Let's talk more about those children who are print novices. These children often like to make up what the story says by looking at the pictures but ignoring the print. They don't realize that the print contains the message. We sometimes say that these readers are "inventing" the story. This is a natural and important step on the path to literacy, as children are establishing that reading makes sense, relies on their language skills, and is enjoyable. Now they need to begin to understand the idea that what they say can be represented by print and what

What does the child know and control?	What is the child ready to learn?
■ Enjoys listening to picture books being read to them ■ Makes connections and loves to talk when listening to a book ■ Knows readers turn the pages of a book ■ Can tell an oral story that may or may not have a beginning, middle, and end ■ Can draw a simple story, usually with one color of crayon ■ May be able to write their first name ■ May or may not know a handful of letters	■ Letter names and sounds ■ Left-to-right directionality across one line of text ■ Voice-to-print matching across one line of text ■ Locating their name in text

FIGURE 3.1
Learners Who Are Ready for Pre-A Texts

they can see in print can be said. As print experts, our eyes naturally gravitate to print. But for a complete novice, it can often be uncomfortable to visually search a sea of black squiggles. Try this. Look at the following story written in a Wingdings font (Figure 3.2) and notice what your eyes do.

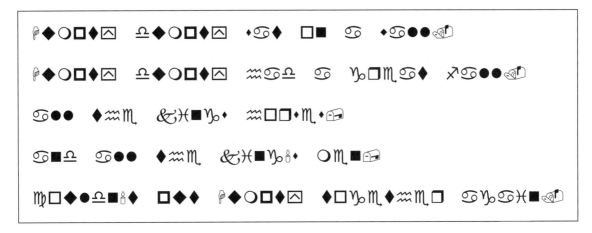

FIGURE 3.2

Did you carefully track the print from right to left or did your eyes wander haphazardly, as you might look at a picture or TV screen? Did you look for something familiar? Did you give up? If you look away now, could you write a letter or a word from the story? Most likely not.

Just as it's very hard for someone who has never been immersed in water to swim, it's hard to jump into a sea of unfamiliar print. Pre-A text is used to help children get their feet wet in print without throwing them in all the way. To help them get acclimated, we can support their learning in the following areas.

Learning How Print Works

The first necessary learning about print is the knowledge that the print contains the message. Children need to become aware that their eyes need to look at the print when they read. The picture is there to support the story, but the print is what is read. Once they understand this, they need to learn how to navigate the print with their eyes. Our print system works from left to right and spaces within the print help us see and hear how our language is separated into words.

Hearing Sounds in Our Language

Phonemic awareness has received a lot of attention in recent years as a critical skill for literacy. In simple terms, it is the ability to hear the component sounds in words. This skill is necessary in order to write new words using their sounds and to read new words by using letter sounds. Typically, around twenty hours of total instruction in phonemic awareness is enough for most children to master the skills. If you divide this by the number of days in one school year, it comes to about seven minutes a day. Also, research shows that phonemic awareness that is taught in conjunction with letters is very effective. This means that writing is the perfect venue for learning about sounds in words (NICHD 2000).

Learning Words

Think back to when you were looking at the Wingdings font. If your name in English was embedded somewhere in the story, your eyes would immediately gravitate to that very familiar island in the sea of unfamiliar print. In early reading, children need these islands of certainty. Having a few known words helps them monitor and keeps their eyes on the print. Names are the obvious place to start because of the high interest factor, but teachers should repeatedly expose new readers to other highly useful words as well.

Learning Letters

Letters and their sounds are the smallest units of our language system. It is critical for children to learn letter names and the various sounds associated with them (Adams 1990). It is not necessary to learn them all before starting to learn to read (Clay 2005b), so our instruction occurs concurrently with reading books and writing stories. We'll use a variety of tools to teach letters, including alphabet books, magnetic letters, writing utensils, iPads, charts, and more. Our goal is letter knowledge that is so automatic that children can focus their brainpower on more complex levels of print.

KEY CHARACTERISTICS OF LEVEL PRE-A TEXTS

To put this very bluntly, most levels are characterized by what the reader *can* do, but Level Pre-A is characterized by what they *can't do yet*. If a child needs Pre-A text, it means that they can't handle Level A because they don't yet understand that the print will give their eyes information. When they have looked at books up to this point, their eyes (and hearts) have been rewarded by studying the pictures, but the black marks have given them very little love. We now need to provide texts that will change this.

When children are unsuccessful with Level A books, it's usually because they can't coordinate their eyes, finger, and mouth in a word-by-word sequence. For our youngest readers, this really is a monumental task if you think about the miniscule eye movement needed to go from one word in a book to the next. And if a child is trying to track with their finger, it's likely that their finger is almost the same size or bigger than the space between the words. These movements are just too small for some children to understand the task. We need to make the movements larger both in terms of space (how far the eyes and finger need to travel to get to the next word) and time (a noticeable pause between the words spoken.) This exaggerated spacing is hard to come by in most published books. The easiest way to provide this type of text is to create it yourself during the lesson with the students. Let's look at how you can create text that makes learning easy in a Pre-A text.

Remember our discussion of the power of emotion and engagement in learning? We need to harness that power to entice young eyes toward print. Children need a payoff for studying print, just like the payoff they get for studying pictures. Consider three factors as you create Pre-A text for your readers.

1. *Story Topics*
   What topics interest children the most? Themselves! Write about things they like, can do, play with, or have. By coauthoring these "stories" with the children's input, you're setting the stage for engagement.
2. *Language Structure*
   Using extremely simple sentence structures will ensure your readers' ability to hold onto the structure while they direct their cognitive efforts toward analyzing the visual component of reading. Sentences of three to five words should work best. Repeat the patterned sentence structure throughout each "story," as we'll explore shortly (see Figure 3.3).
3. *Print Information*
   The print needs to pop right off the page. Starting sentences with the children's names will help with this because if they are familiar with any print at all, it will be their name and will be of high interest (Cunningham 1988). You are going for stark contrast against the white paper, so use dark, thick-tipped markers. Exaggerate letter size and the space between words. Make it easy for young eyes to see that groups of letters make words.

CHAPTER 3

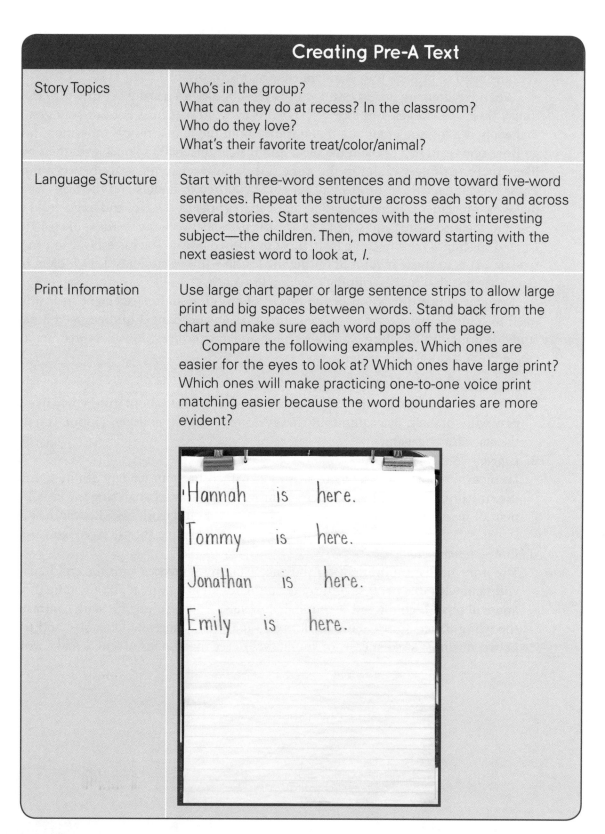

Creating Pre-A Text	
Story Topics	Who's in the group? What can they do at recess? In the classroom? Who do they love? What's their favorite treat/color/animal?
Language Structure	Start with three-word sentences and move toward five-word sentences. Repeat the structure across each story and across several stories. Start sentences with the most interesting subject—the children. Then, move toward starting with the next easiest word to look at, *I*.
Print Information	Use large chart paper or large sentence strips to allow large print and big spaces between words. Stand back from the chart and make sure each word pops off the page. 　Compare the following examples. Which ones are easier for the eyes to look at? Which ones have large print? Which ones will make practicing one-to-one voice print matching easier because the word boundaries are more evident?

Hannah   is   here.

Tommy   is   here.

Jonathan   is   here.

Emily   is   here.

FIGURE 3.3
Creating Pre-A Text

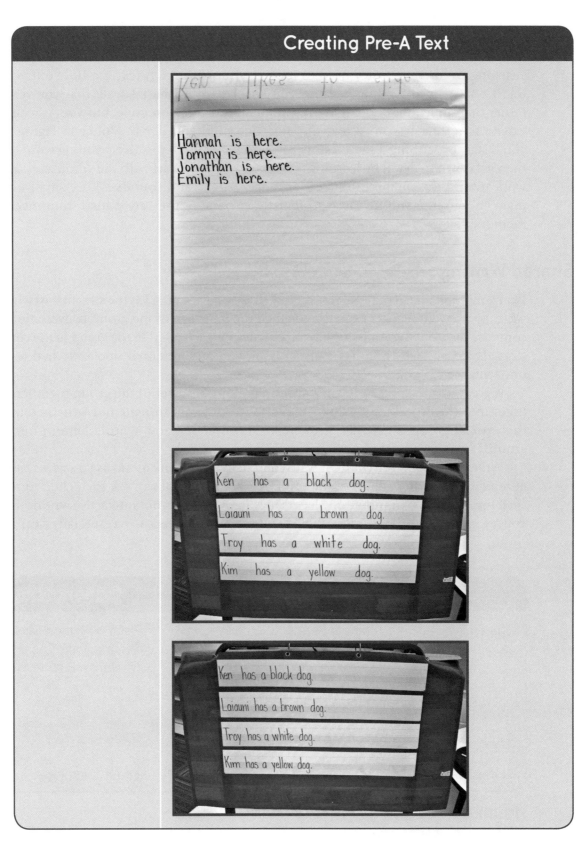

FIGURE 3.3 (*Continued*)

TEACHING WITH TEACHER-CREATED PRE-A TEXT

Teaching children that they need to look at print with Pre-A text is a little different from traditional guided reading because you will be using shared texts that you've created, rather than individual books. We recommend a two-lesson cycle, but you, of course, can extend to a three-lesson cycle if that fits your children's needs. Notice in Figure 3.4 that you'll start by scribing a shared story on chart paper, then practice pointing word by word, then get down to detail by learning words, then letters. Start with the whole message, then work toward the smallest units of language, letters, and sounds. Those small units will make more sense and be easier to remember because they are pulled from meaningful, memorable text.

Shared Writing

Plan your topic ahead of time. You should already have a plan for the structure of what you'll write, so use your teacher expertise to guide the language of the group conversation as you compose the story. Typically, we have a sentence for each child in the group in the completed story. This way each child has a visual hook and an emotional hook attached to at least one sentence.

A great first lesson can revolve around making a poster of the group members. Invite them into the process by saying, "We're so lucky to get to read and write together with this special group of friends. Let's make sure we all know who is here in our special group!"

Write the story as the children watch and help you. Think aloud as you write, calling the group's attention to features of the print. For example, you can ask each child to help you spell their name or contribute any letters they know. (This is not interactive writing, however. You are going to do all the transcribing because the print needs to be especially clear and well

Day 1	Day 2	Optional Day 3
Shared Writing	Point & Reread Shared Writing Sentence Puzzles	Point & Reread Shared Writing and/or Assemble Sentence Puzzles.
Point & Read	Point & Read	
Word Learning	Word Learning	Word Learning
Letter Learning	Letter Learning	Letter Learning

FIGURE 3.4
Pre-A Lesson Cycle

sized.) You can stretch words and notice the first sound. You can also notice out loud that every time you write *is* it looks the same! Amazing!

Allie	is	here.
Brandy	is	here.
Cameron	is	here.
Dwayne	is	here.

You will return to these stories in future lessons and, later, as an option for familiar reading. You can even post them or keep them available for your children to read at other times of the day.

Point and Read

Lead the group in jointly pointing to each word as you read together. Position the chart so every child can reach it and touch each word. The goal here is to coordinate eyes, fingers, and mouths. Talk to them about this. Tell them what to look at when their finger points to each word. Read the story a few times. Remember, since the goal here is to coordinate their eyes, fingers, and mouths, this isn't the time for fluency practice. You should read very slowly, with obvious pauses between words. As this routine becomes familiar, you can switch things up. You might let individual children point while the group reads, invite partners to point together as the group reads, or ask the children to point while you read. As long as you keep in mind the ultimate goal of learning to keep their eyes on the print, you can be flexible in the pointing and reading.

Not only are you teaching how print works, but you're also teaching the beginnings of phonological awareness. Before children can hear the component sounds in words, they need to be able to hear component words within language. As you read slowly, separating out the words, you will be demonstrating how to hear increasingly smaller units of language. Ehri and Sweet's work (1991) showed us how hearing the sounds in speech aid in learning to match one-to-one.

Sentence Puzzles

In Lesson 2, the group will explore looking at print and practicing one-to-one matching even more explicitly by putting cut-up parts of sentences from their story back together (Figure 3.5). Using either large sentence strips or strips of tagboard, write one sentence from the story for each child. The first few times, you might have the children read each sentence, as you cut it word by word. After they know the drill, you may have the sentences precut and placed in envelopes. The children will reassemble their sentences from left to right, then reread them, matching their eyes, finger, and voice. As students work, make sure they leave spaces between the words and make sure you check each child to see if they are beginning to match voice to print.

Word Learning

Decide what word in the story might be a good word for closer examination. Almost always at first, it will be students' own names. Use a variety of materials to help children explore their new word. For example, if you've chosen to focus on their names, you can give each child a baggie with the magnetic letters they need to make their name, you might give them

FIGURE 3.5
Landon is assembling his cut up story. Putting together sentence puzzles helps children focus on early print concepts.

FIGURE 3.6
Alyssa is putting her name puzzle together using her name template. This helps her learn words are made up of letters in a certain order.

a template of their names to either place their letters on or under, you could have them practice writing their name on white boards, or you may make name puzzles out of tag board (Figure 3.6). Use your creativity! To make sure you are helping them code this word several ways in their brain—they should be hearing the word, saying the word, seeing the word, and either writing or building the word. Very soon these readers will be learning how the letters in the words relate to the sounds their mouths make and can be used as anchors when they're reading.

Afterward, make sure you have them return to the story and find the word they have been learning. Let them see how it fits into the story. This way, we take the word out of context, examine it, and then return it to context again. This is important in two ways. Not only does it make remembering the words easier, it also sends the message that meaning is our purpose. We don't learn random words for random reasons. We learn them to help us read and write meaningful stories.

One more caution about word learning at this level: Our goal here is for children to learn to keep their eyes on the print and to take the first steps toward understanding one-to-one matching. It can be tempting to think that children need to learn a large core of words before they move into Level A books, but that would hold our kids back from books for too long. The time spent using Pre-A text is meant to help them know where to look, to begin learning about one-to-one matching, to learn a few hooks in print by becoming familiar with a few words, and to learn some letters. We want our kids in books as soon as possible.

Letter Learning

Finally, every lesson should include work on learning letters. Here, we need to make an important distinction between *instructional activities that teach* and *instructional activities that provide practice*. Sometimes we forget the explicit teaching and move right into practice. For example, naming letters or using flashcards are *practice* activities, not *teaching* activities. For print newbies, we need to provide instruction that helps them notice the little details that distinguish one letter from another. What makes a *t* different from an *l*? What makes a *c* different from an *o*? What parts are similar? What's the fastest way to write an *h*? Once you've explicitly *taught* the details of a new letter, then the *practice* activities become appropriate. We'll use both explicit teaching and practice activities in guided reading because children need to learn new letters and they need to practice those letters that are partially known so they can become known automatically.

For this portion of the lesson, choose from some of the following teaching procedures, based on your children's needs. Remember, when you're introducing a new letter to the group, it's important to choose from the *teaching procedures* we recommend. When you're ready to firm up known and partially known letters, the *practice procedures* listed will fit the bill.

Materials

- Create an **alphabet book** for each child. We prefer to make these easily by binding tagboard into a book and writing in the letters. But, if you prefer, you can also purchase alphabet books that are premade especially for this purpose, or you can find several nice options online. Whether you make them, buy them, or download them, these alphabet books should follow these guidelines:
  - Each page should feature a clear model of the upper- and lower-case letter, with a simple, clear picture of a word that links to the sound of that letter.
  - The letters should be large enough for a child to trace the letter with their finger.
  - The picture should be something that can't be confused with something else. For instance, we suggest avoiding *alligator* for *a* because kids will call it a *crocodile* half the time.
  - Keep the book very simple and free from unnecessary visual distractions (see Figure 3.7).
- Keep a large collection of **magnetic letters** in various bright colors. You can organize them in plastic boxes or magnetic trays like cookie sheets (see Figure 3.8).
- Have small **plastic baggies**, so each child can have a collection of letters to work with during the lesson (Figure 3.9).
- Keep a variety of **writing materials** for children to use when practicing letter formation. White boards, chalk boards, and paper are all great. Use your imagination.

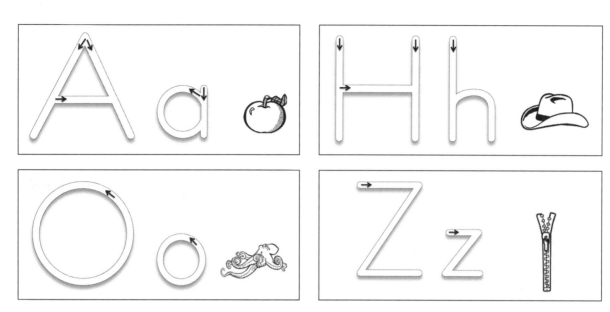

FIGURE 3.7
Sample Pages from an ABC Book

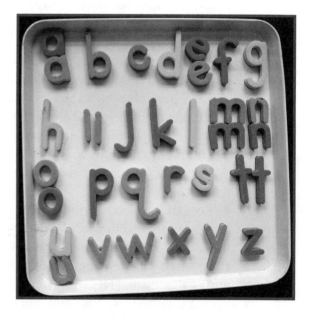

FIGURE 3.8
Magnetic Letter Storage

FIGURE 3.9
Individual Magnetic Letter Baggies

Procedures for Teaching a New Letter

- Choose high utility letters (ones that occur frequently) and the first letters of students' names. Even the names of friends are highly interesting to young children, so teach the first letter of the name of each group member. Most schools follow a sequence for letter introduction and it's fine to follow this if it makes sense, but don't try to keep up with the same timeframe as the whole class. Small groups exist precisely so you can go at their own pace and teach what they need when they need it.

- Introduce the letter by connecting it to a word, for example, "We're going to learn about the letter *S* because it's the first letter in Sara's name!"
- Open the alphabet books to the target letter's page. Model tracing the letter as you verbalize how to form the letter, then name it. *"Start at the top, around, down, a."* Practice this several times with all students verbalizing the formation and naming the letter. Explain to students that they need to tell their hand what to do. Children only need to know how their hand should move so keep this verbalization simple to make the task clear.
- Transfer this new learning to writing. On whiteboards or paper, have students practice the new letter, while verbalizing the formation and naming it.

Procedures for Practicing Known and Partially Known Letters

- Read the alphabet book. Choral read, partner read, individual read. Read every letter or just the known and partially known letters. When reading, name the letter, then the picture, then make the sound. *"S, s, sun, /s/."*
- Give each child a baggie with a variety of known and partially known magnetic letters. Have them name the letters. One option is to have baggies with an assortment of different letters, both uppercase and lowercase. Another option is to have baggies that have just a few different letters but multiples of those letters.
- Race the Teacher to write and name the target letter four times. You will write (and name) the target letter on a whiteboard, while your students try to race you by writing and naming the letter four times before you do. You should write slowly enough to model careful writing and to allow them to win (sometimes!).
- Roll and Record is a game that allows children to practice letter naming automaticity and proper letter formation. On a blank die, write one letter on each side that a child knows but needs to control with automaticity. Provide a 6-by-9-inch piece of 1-inch grid paper. This allows one column for each letter on the die. As the child rolls the die, they should name the letter fast and write it quickly on the grid paper in the correct column. They continue rolling, naming, and writing, until the time is up for the portion of the lesson or their sheet is filled up with letters (see Figure 3.10).

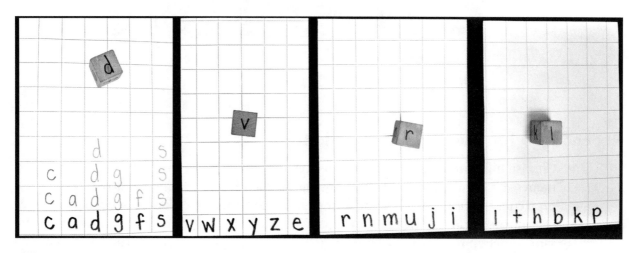

FIGURE 3.10
Roll and Record

Remember to check out our correlating Literacy Center ideas that support the work students are doing at the small group table with teacher created Pre-A texts. www.stenhouse.com/content/intentional-from-the-start

REMEMBER THE PURPOSE OF TEACHING WITH PRE-A TEXT

Guided reading has always been about supporting children as they read books. Using teacher-created Pre-A text is a scaffold that we put in place to teach children the skills they need to begin to navigate Level A. Those skills include putting their eyes on the print and attempting to search for information. They also include shaky one-to-one matching. As soon as you feel your group might be ready to move into Level A books, do it! Your kids don't need to wait until they're reading Pre-A texts perfectly and you can expect errors when they first move into Level A. They may invent at first. They may add more words than they see on the page. Expect this and teach through it. Mostly likely, if you have taught explicitly with Pre-A text, those behaviors will quickly come under control. Use your judgment as your best guide. When you think your group is ready, go for it. Think back to our novice swimmers. Moving into Level A is like just taking your hands off the swimmer for a minute and letting them try out their floaties to see if they actually will hold them up. The swimmer will squirm for a second and possibly have a bit of panic. But once they see that they aren't sinking, they relax and enjoy the beginnings of independence. We'll talk in the next chapter about how to help your readers through that first bit of panic when they open a Level A book for the first time and begin their journey of reading *real* books.

EXAMPLE LESSON WITH TEACHER-CREATED PRE-A TEXT

We've explored the big ideas of teaching with Pre-A texts. We know our purpose is to get children's eyes on print, learn letters, and help their ears to hear the sounds in language. With all of this in mind, let's join Mrs. Jones at the small group table to observe a lesson focused on Pre-A text. See Figure 3.11.

DAY 1	**Component:** Shared Writing **Focus:** Noticing that what is spoken can be written
	Mrs. Jones decides to have a conversation about what the children like to do while they are at school. The children talk about liking to build, paint, play, and read. Mrs. Jones has a large piece of chart paper ready so she can write the "story" as they construct it together.

FIGURE 3.11
Pre-A Lesson Using a Teacher Created Text

CHAPTER 3

DAY 1 (Continued)

Student and Teacher Interactions	Teacher Moves and Rationale
Mrs. Jones: Let's write a story today about what we like to do at school. Karie said she likes to build so we are going to write: Karie likes to build. Watch me write her name. **Mrs. Jones:** Karie, did I get your name right? **Karie:** K-a-r-i-e. Yes, that's right.	Mrs. Jones writes Karie's name on the chart paper.
Mrs. Jones: Now, I need to leave a space before I write the word *likes*. I am going to say the word *likes* slowly as I write it. Can you say it slowly with me?	Mrs. Jones leaves an exaggerated space after Karie's name. She does this so the children can see where one word ends and the next one begins.
Group: lllllllliiiiiiiiiikessssss.	Mrs. Jones writes the word as the group says it slowly together.
Mrs. Jones: Let's read what we wrote so we know what word comes next. **Group**: Karie likes to . . .	Mrs. Jones models precise pointing to the words from left to right as the group reads the text slowly.
Mrs. Jones: *to* is the next word I need to write. /t/, /t/, /t/ *to*, *to* starts like turtle on our ABC chart, so I am going to leave a space and write a *t*. Watch me finish writing *to*.	Mrs. Jones leaves an exaggerated space and then writes the letter *t*. Since her goal is to model isolating the initial sound she writes in the *o* for the group.
Mrs. Jones: Let's read again. **Group:** Karie likes to build.	Mrs. Jones points to the words while the group reads together.
Mrs. Jones: /b/, /b/, /b/ build, *build* starts like bear so I am going to leave a space and write a *b*. Now say *build* slowly with me while I write the rest of the word. **Group:** buiiiiiiilllllld.	Mrs. Jones leaves an exaggerated space, writes the letter *b* and then writes the rest of the word while the children say it together slowly.
Mrs. Jones: Let's read the sentence about Karie while I point to the words. **Group:** Karie likes to build.	Mrs. Jones points precisely to the words as the group reads the sentence together.
	Mrs. Jones continues in this same manner writing one sentence for each child in the small group. She writes each sentence in a different color.

FIGURE 3.11 (*Continued*)

Component: Point and Read
Focuses: Look at print; left-to right-directionality; match voice to print

Mrs. Jones has the children stand in front of the story they just wrote so they can read it together. While they read the text together, she will model left to right directionality and one-to-one voice-to-print matching. She encourages the children to point, look, and read along with her.

Student and Teacher Interactions	Teacher Moves and Rationale
Mrs. Jones: Everyone put your finger here under Karie's name. Your finger helps your eyes know where to look. Now let's point and read. **Group:** Karie . . . likes . . . to . . . build. Aubrey . . . likes . . . to . . . paint. Johnny . . . likes . . . to . . . play. E.J. . . . likes . . . to . . . read.	Mrs. Jones is careful to model precise pointing to match her voice to the text, reading slowly and methodically. This support encourages children to point precisely too.

Mrs. Jones knows a child's name is the most important word to them as they begin their reading and writing journey. So, she has each child locate their name in the text one at a time. Next, even though the children are print novices, Mrs. Jones knows it is never too early to have them focus on locating high frequency words with support. So, she decides to have the children locate *likes* and *to* together.

Mrs. Jones: Now, everyone point to the word *likes*. What word did you find? **Group:** *likes* **Mrs. Jones:** Can you find the word *to*? (All the children point to the word *to*.) That's right! You found the word *to*! Now let's read the story one more time with our fingers and our eyes.	
Group: Karie . . . likes . . . to . . . build. Aubrey . . . likes . . . to . . . paint. Johnny . . . likes . . . to . . . play. E.J. . . . likes . . . to . . . read.	After finding words in isolation, Mrs. Jones has the group put it all together and read the entire text again.

FIGURE 3.11 (*Continued*)

CHAPTER 3

DAY 1 (Continued)

Component: Word Learning
Focus: Learn a few helpful words

During her prep period, Mrs. Jones got magnetic boards ready with magnetic letters so each child can build their own name. She also placed the letters *t* and *o* in baggies to build the word *to*.

Student and Teacher Interactions	Teacher Moves and Rationale
Mrs. Jones: On your white board are the letters in your name. Make your name with the letters on the board. (Students work independently to make their name.)	
Mrs. Jones: Johnny, what word did you make? **Johnny:** I made my name *Johnny*. **Mrs. Jones:** Check it with your finger and your eyes, does it look right? **Johnny:** Joooohnnnny, yep! It looks right. **Mrs. Jones:** Nice job Johnny, making your name quickly so it looks right! Mix it up and make it again.	Mrs. Jones wants the "checking routine" to become well established. So, she has each child point and run their finger under their name as they read it. Mrs. Jones repeats the same process with all the children and their names.
Mrs. Jones: We needed the word *to* to write our story. Let's learn that word! What's the first letter? Can you hear it? /t/ /t/ /t/, it starts like *turtle* so take the letter *t* out of your baggie. (Children find the letter *t* and put it on their boards.)	Mrs. Jones hands out the baggies with letters to make the word *to*. Using the ABC chart, Mrs. Jones models saying a letter sound, linking it to the correct picture cue, and locating the letter needed to start the word *to*.
Mrs. Jones: Now comes the letter *o*. Take the *o* out of the bag and place it next to the *t* so it looks like the word *to*. (Children grab the *o* and finish making the word *to*.)	
Mrs. Jones: E.J., can you find the word *to* in your sentence in the story? (E.J. quickly finds the word *to*.) Yeah! You found the word *to*! Now let's read your sentence again.	Mrs. Jones returns to the story to locate the word *to* and read each child's sentence. Mrs. Jones repeats this process with all the students.

FIGURE 3.11   (*Continued*)

Component: Letter Learning
Focus: Learn letters and names

Daily tracing of the ABC book has helped students in the past to learn the letters and letter sounds quickly. So, Mrs. Jones makes this a part of the letter-learning routine before turning their attention to learning a new letter.

Student and Teacher Interactions	Teacher Moves and Rationale
Mrs. Jones: Time to practice our ABC Book. Open your books to the letter *Aa* and get your finger ready to trace the letter. (Mrs. Jones waits until everyone has their finger ready to trace the uppercase *A*). **Group:** A, a, apple, /a/; B, b, bear, /b/; C, c, cat, /k/ . . . Z, z, zipper, /z/.	Mrs. Jones adds her voice to the ABC book reading until she feels the children can support each other as they read.

Mrs. Jones decides to spend a little time learning the new letter *k* because Karie's name starts with *K* and it's also in *likes* from their story. She shows them a magnetic letter *k* and then has them look in the shared text to locate *likes*. Afterwards, she shows them how to write the letter *k* with correct letter formation.

Mrs. Jones: Let's learn how to write the letter *k*. Watch me write *k* on the board and listen to the words I say as I write it: ▪ start at the top; ▪ down; ▪ slant in; ▪ slant out; ▪ *k*.	Mrs. Jones models writing the letter *k* large on the white board. She gives the language for how to correctly write the letter *k*. She'll call for the children to say these words when they practice writing the letter *k* too.
Mrs. Jones: Now you write the letter *k* in the air as I write it on the board again: start at the top, down; slant in; slant out; *k*.	Mrs. Jones has the children write it in the air because it is kinesthetic and involves big body movements.
Mrs. Jones: Now write the letter *k* on your board. Say the words with me as you write it. **Group**: Start at the top, down; slant in; slant out; *k*.	Mrs. Jones watches the children carefully to make sure they are starting at the top of the letter and writing it correctly. She stops anyone who begins their letter *k* in the wrong spot. To help with correct formation she may: ▪ help a child by doing hand over hand to write the letter *k*.

FIGURE 3.11   (*Continued*)

DAY 1 (Continued)

Mrs. Jones: Make it again! (Students write the letter *k* several more times on their board and name it each time.)

- quickly make a *dotted k* for a child to trace.
- point to where a child should start writing the letter *k*.

This decision will be based on what she knows about the children at her table and their fine motor skills, motor planning skills, and language skills.

DAY 2

Components: Point and Reread Shared Writing and Sentence Puzzle
Focus: Look at print; left-to-right directionality; voice-to-print matching

Mrs. Jones begins the lesson by having the group reread the story they composed from the previous lesson. Once again, she has the group stand in front of the chart paper and point to each word as they read the story together. After reading it, she is prepared to have the children put their sentence puzzles together.

Student and Teacher Interactions

Mrs. Jones: I have written each of your parts of the story on a strip of paper. E.J., here is your part of the story. You read it while I cut it up into a puzzle.
E.J.: E.J. . . . likes . . . to . . . read.
Mrs. Jones: Karie, your turn.
Karie: Karie . . . likes . . . to . . . build.
Mrs. Jones: Aubrey?
Aubrey: Aubrey . . . likes . . . to . . . paint.
Mrs. Jones: Johnny, your turn.
Johnny: Johnny . . . likes . . . to . . . play.

Teacher Moves and Rationale

Mrs. Jones cuts each word off the strip as each child reads their sentence. While she gives them the direction to put it back together, she arranges the words in a vertical list to their right. This will allow them to assemble the puzzle by bringing the words into their line of vision in a left-to-right manner.

Mrs. Jones: Perfect! Now I want you to put your part of the story back together again. What word will you find first?
Group: My name!
Mrs. Jones: Right! That's easy because it's your name! Start your sentence, with your name, right here. (Each child slides their name to where Mrs. Jones pointed.)

When each child grabs their name, Mrs. Jones gets them started in the right direction by showing them where to put it on the left.

FIGURE 3.11   (*Continued*)

CHAPTER 3

DAY 2 (Continued)

Each time the children add a word to their sentence, Mrs. Jones has them go back, point to the words, and read to find the next word.

Mrs. Jones: Now, what word comes next? Let's read together to find out. Point to your sentence. **Group:** E.J./Karie/Aubrey/Johnny . . . likes.	If needed, Mrs. Jones points to help support voice-to-print matching.
Mrs. Jones: Yes! The next word is *likes*. /lllllllll/ikes. *Likes* begins with the letter *l*. Can you find the word that starts with an *l*? (Everyone correctly locates the word *likes*.)	If someone is uncertain about what the letter *l* looks like, Mrs. Jones is prepared to show the magnetic letter *l* to support their searching.
Mrs. Jones: Correct, put the word *likes* right here. Let's read it again together to figure out what comes next. **Group:** E.J./Karie/Aubrey/Johnny . . . likes . . . to . . .	Mrs. Jones shows everyone right where to slide the word *likes*. She purposely leaves space between the two words to encourage voice-to-print matching.
Mrs. Jones: *To* is the next word. It's the short word we learned to read and write yesterday. It begins with a *t*. Can you find the word *to*? (Everyone easily locates the word *to*.)	
Mrs. Jones: That's right. Put the word *to* right here. Let's point and read it again. Now, remember, each of you has a different thing you like to do at school so each of your words will be different. **Group**: E.J./Karie/Aubrey/Johnny . . . likes . . . to . . . read/build/paint/play.	Mrs. Jones points out where to put the word *to*.
Mrs. Jones: The next word is easy to find because it's your last word in your sentence. Put it right here.	Mrs. Jones points to where to put their last word.
Mrs. Jones: Now you point to each word and read your sentence again. (Everyone points to and reads their part of the story.) **Mrs. Jones:** Nice job pointing to each word while you read your parts of the story!	Mrs. Jones monitors as everyone points to their sentence.

FIGURE 3.11   (*Continued*)

Component: Point and Read
Focuses: Look at print; left-to-right directionality; match voice to print

Mrs. Jones brings the children back to the text on the chart paper once again. It gives the children an opportunity to move a bit and redirects their attention back to the entire text. This time, they each point to the part of the story that is about them. Mrs. Jones stands at the ready to support anyone who needs help with directionality or voice-to-print matching.

Student and Teacher Interactions	Teacher Moves and Rationale
Mrs. Jones: Karie, you get to point and read first because your part of the story is first. Get your finger ready! **Karie**: Karie . . . likes . . . to . . . build. (Karie points to each word correctly.)	
Aubrey: Aubrey likes to paint. (Aubrey slides her finger from left to right without precise pointing.) **Mrs. Jones**: Aubrey, watch me point to each word as I read it. Aubrey . . . likes . . . to . . . paint. Now you try it and make it match. **Aubrey:** Aubrey . . . likes . . . to . . . paint. **Mrs. Jones:** There you go! That time you made it match! Your turn Johnny.	Mrs. Jones models voice-to-print matching and invites Aubrey to try again.

Johnny and E.J. both point and read their parts of the story with precision. Mrs. Jones praises their efforts to point, match, and read. She has the group finish this portion of the lesson by reading the entire text again while she points to the words.

Component: Word Learning
Focus: Learn a few helpful words

Mrs. Jones decides to have the children each practice the letters in their own name using their name puzzles.

Student and Teacher Interactions	Teacher Moves and Rationale
Mrs. Jones: Here are your baggies with your name puzzles in them. Dump out the letters and put your names together. What letter will you grab first?	Mrs. Jones watches the children carefully as they assemble their puzzles. Depending on what the children know

FIGURE 3.11   (*Continued*)

Karie: K!

E.J.: E!

Johnny: Hmmmm, this one.

Mrs. Jones: Right Johnny, that's the letter *J*.

Aubrey: A!

Mrs. Jones: Now put the rest of your name puzzle together. If you forget what letter comes next what can you do?

Aubrey: Look at the label on the baggie.

E.J. Grab your name card.

Mrs. Jones: Both of those are good ideas if you forget what comes next.

about the letters in their name, she might prompt with:

- What is the next letter?
- Are you right?
- Something doesn't look right; can you fix it?
- Is this letter or this letter next?

After the children put their name puzzles together, she has them check to see if it looks right by sliding their finger under their name from left to right while their eyes look across the word too. She also has them practice writing, checking, and reading their name on their whiteboards several times before turning their attention to letter learning.

Component: Letter Learning
Focus: Learn letters and names

Prior to the lesson, Mrs. Jones prepares a baggie of magnetic letters for each child. In them are the upper case and lowercase letters of each letter in their name. To support their new learning about the letter *Kk*, Mrs. Jones also puts an upper- and lowercase version in the baggie. Mrs. Jones plans to have each child point to and name each letter from left to right across the line of letters.

Mrs. Jones: Let's finish our time together by practicing some letters. In your baggie are the letters in your name. I have also added the new letter, *Kk*, we learned yesterday. Dump them out and line them up like this.

(Mrs. Jones randomly lines up the letters in Karie's name in a horizontal line in front of her.)

Mrs. Jones: Karie, since I did yours for you, would you start here and name the letters in your line?

Karie: e, r, K, A, r, I, R, E, a, k, i

Mrs. Jones: You did a great job naming all your letters! Now let's see if E.J. can name his. Start right here.

FIGURE 3.11 *(Continued)*

DAY 2 (Continued)

E.J.: Mrs. Jones, that's easy! I only have a few letters! J, k, e, K, j, E.

Mrs. Jones: Yes, you do E.J. Your name's very short! We're going to have to add some extra letters to your baggie. Let's see about Johnny. Can you start right here and name the letters?

Johnny: N, y, O, h, n, j, Y, n, o, K, H, N, k, J. I remembered the first letter in my name Mrs. Jones! I practiced it at home last night!

Mrs. Jones: Yay! I bet you'll never forget the name of that letter again. Alright, Aubrey, you're the last one. Start here and name your letters.

Aubrey: I can name them superfast! R, y, A, u, B, E, k, a, r, b, K, Y, U, e!

Mrs. Jones knows this task is getting easier for them to do and everyone is ready for new letters to be introduced into their baggie of letters. She will be doing this for the next set of lessons. They finish this day's lesson by matching the uppercase letters in their baggies with the lowercase letters. Mrs. Jones encourages the children to name the letter as they make matches fast because it is one more way to build automaticity.

FIGURE 3.11

Learning How to Look at Print

Mrs. Jones has been looking over her lesson notes from her group working with Pre-A texts. She notices that Karie, Aubrey, Johnny, and E.J. have all made progress. The deliberate reading and writing work with their names has taught them that the "squiggles" carry the important message and the pictures support the reading. They have trained their eyes where to look when reading and now their instruction needs to focus on *how* to look at print.

All four children are able to locate and read their own name in print. E.J., Johnny, and Karie can write their names independently without a model or teacher prompt. Aubrey can recognize and name the letters in her name in isolation. However, she struggles to remember the order of the letters when attempting to write it on her work throughout the day. She is resourceful and knows where she can go in the classroom to independently get a model to copy. Mrs. Jones knows learning their names is the gateway into the process of learning high frequency words.

Aubrey and Johnny now know twenty-five to twenty-seven letters consistently, with few lapses. Although Karie and E.J. are taking on letters more quickly than Aubrey and Johnny, they are inconsistent and slow when recalling letter names. They both solidly know thirty to thirty-five letters and inconsistently know ten more.

From her notes and based on research, she knows it is time to start working in text levels A and B. She can't wait until her students know all the letter names and letter sounds to move into real books. It would be a waste of precious learning time. She knows her students are ready to learn:

➤ how to look at print.

➤ some high utility, high frequency words.

➤ more letter names and letter sounds.

Now you've had a peek into Mrs. Jones's analysis of her lesson notes. If you are good at taking notes while you teach, these observations can provide a wealth of information. Your notes can give you an idea of what a child is thinking and doing as they interact with texts, words, and letters. They can also help you to answer the two important questions: What does the child know and control? What is the child ready to learn? Let's look at the questions through the lens of readers who are ready to engage with text levels A and B (see Figure 4.1).

We're sure you've noticed there are only slight differences between this chart and the one we presented at the beginning of the last chapter. This is purposeful. The child working at the Pre-A level is not much different than the child ready to work in levels A and B. You only need to spend enough time working at the Pre-A level for a child to learn where to look, how to read and write their name, and some letter names and sounds. Move to text levels A and B as soon as you can, so you can avoid wasting a child's learning time working on what they already know and control. These same skills will continue to be practiced and built upon in later levels.

What does the child know and control?	What is the child ready to learn?
▪ Enjoys listening to picture books being read aloud	▪ Left-to-right directionality across one line of text
▪ Makes connections and loves to talk when listening to a book	▪ One-to-one voice-to-print matching
▪ Knows readers turn the pages of a book	▪ High frequency words
▪ With support, can tell an oral story that has a beginning, middle, and end	▪ Letter names and sounds
▪ Can draw a simple story and is beginning to use a variety of colors	▪ Return sweep on two lines of text
▪ Usually can write their first name	
▪ Knows twenty or more letters, maybe with lapses	
▪ Knows print contains the message	
▪ Can locate their name in print	

FIGURE 4.1
Learners Who Are Ready for Levels A and B Texts

MY CHILDREN'S EYES ARE ON THE PRINT. NOW WHAT?

In Chapter 3, we explored the big ideas of teaching with a teacher-created Pre-A text. Our goal was to get our readers' eyes to look at the print and to help them realize a book's message would be revealed through the writing on the page. Of course, that's not all we accomplished with Pre-A text. We modeled left-to-right movement, one-to-one matching of spoken and printed words, and listening to the component sounds that make up our speech. It would be really easy if we could have a simple checklist for each level that would indicate that one level was mastered and those skills were complete. In reality, becoming literate is messier and more complex than that. We need to help children develop skills across levels as we model, support, and allow for mistakes during independent practice. For this reason, it's important to avoid thinking about children as levels (Lisa is a Level B) and start thinking in terms of what children are ready to learn next and which books will provide those opportunities. With this in mind, consider what children will be ready to learn next, once they know the print is what they need to examine with their eyes. We'll support them in the following areas.

Learning How Print Works

We used Pre-A text to lure children's eyes from the picture to the print to find the message. Now we need to lure their eyes into the firm habit of scanning print left to right. When we created Pre-A texts, we modeled this behavior when we wrote in front of the children and when we pointed as we read. We allowed our young readers to join in, by group pointing and then taking individual turns pointing left to right while reading. We put together cut-up sentences, word by word, left to right. After all this modeling and scaffolding, our children are now ripe for consolidating this learning in books on their own. We'll use Levels A and B for lots of practice in independently moving left to right across print. A new skill will include the return left sweep when we introduce books that have more than one line of print on each page, usually in Level B books. As with most skills, what was modeled and heavily scaffolded in one level will be firmed up and practiced independently in the next band of levels.

Matching each spoken word to a printed word is another must-learn at this point. Like directional behavior, one-to-one matching was modeled and scaffolded in Pre-A. Now it's time to work for independence. You've probably seen children at various stages of understanding one-to-one matching. At first many children can match only patterned sentences that contain only one-syllable words. Multisyllable words throw them off. Or they can match until the pattern changes, and then they invent a story of their own. This is all normal development, but we use Levels A and B to tighten up these skills. We start with the simplest Level A books and then progress through books with more print, less pattern, and multiple lines of print. Learning high frequency words makes this a much easier burden on the eyes, so we'll focus on that more in this chapter.

Hearing Sounds in Our Language and Beginning to Match Sounds to Print

Solving unknown words in reading and writing is impossible without understanding the link between sound and print (Ehri 2004). The first step is the ability to hear the individual and clustered sounds that make up words. Although we don't do much isolated segmenting of phonemes in our guided reading lessons, we do practice phonemic awareness in every lesson with early readers. We stretch the sounds in words whenever we want to write a new word. We might listen for chunks of sounds by clapping the syllables in our names. We elongate and sometimes isolate first sounds or last sounds or chunks of sounds in words throughout our lessons. Because guided reading is all about authentic practice of skills, we try to connect our work with phonemic awareness to reading and writing the texts we use in our lessons.

Learning Words

When we created Pre-A text, we used children's names as magnets for their eyes. We need more magnets in print at this point, and Levels A and B answer this need with high frequency words. These words are called "high frequency" for an obvious reason—they occur frequently. We don't want cognitive energy used to solve and re-solve these words every time they are encountered, so children need to learn how to learn new words, so some of what they read can be known with automatic responses. Devoting some time in guided reading to learning high frequency words is very important for our earliest readers. We want children using every tool they have to learn these words, by using any letter sounds they know and remembering the other parts if necessary.

Learning Letters

You may have readers who need to read in Levels A and B books who know the names and sounds of all the letters. You may also have readers in Levels A and B who know only a few letter names. Eventually, all readers need automatic knowledge of letter names, sounds, alternate sounds, and common clusters. You'll continue with some of the same letter-learning activities done previously, and you'll add expectations of faster responses, more flexibility, and reciprocal knowledge in both reading and writing.

KEY CHARACTERISTICS OF LEVELS A AND B TEXTS

You make many decisions in every guided reading lesson, but perhaps the most important decision you make is your choice of book. Remember it's like the swim teacher choosing the right water for their developing swimmer. It needs to be just right to support the skill level of the learner. To make a good choice, we're going to encourage you to look for book characteristics, rather than just picking a book from a certain level. We'll guide you to the levels where you are most likely to find those characteristics; remain flexible, however, and don't limit yourself to one level.

For children who are ready to practice directionality and one-to-one matching, your Levels A and B books usually will be your best bets. As you select titles, keep in mind your main goals. You want your readers to have an easy time seeing the print, keeping their eyes on the print, and scanning the print in an organized left-to-right fashion. You want the book to support them in seeing each word distinctly, with room enough for their finger to point under each word. You want the sentence structures to be easy for their brain to hold on to while they spend cognitive energy trying to match each spoken word to a printed word. Books that will support these goals typically have these common characteristics.

- Print is on the left page, with the picture on the right page. Though not necessary for all their books, this format allows children to consciously decide to put their eyes on the print and makes it easier to keep them there. When print and picture are in closer proximity, it's very tempting for the eyes to wander around in a disorganized way. Readers quickly learn to keep their eyes on the print in a variety of formats, but for the earliest readers, we can help them resist the temptation to "read" while their eyes aren't on the print.

- The font is clear, simple, and large. As children become more automatic and flexible with letter forms, they can handle a variety of interesting fonts. At first though, we need to make it easy for them to recognize what they know. Even changing fonts from a Zaner Bloser® style or to traditional Times New Roman printed *a* or *g* (see Figure 4.2) can make a word hard to recognize for a novice. Thinking about details like this can make a difference for many readers.

- Print is limited to just one or two lines. When children can handle one line of print, look for books with two lines of print. Two or more lines of print mean the child will have to learn to "return sweep" and start the second line on the left. If you aren't having children point as they read, you might be surprised to find the creative directional patterns some children use. Watch to be sure directional behavior is secured with all your early readers.

- Words are separated by exaggerated spaces. This helps in a couple of ways. First, the spacing makes it easier visually to see where one word ends and another begins. Take a look back at the Wingding text in Chapter 3 (page 29) and notice how much effort it takes to differentiate one word from another because the spacing is so minute. You want readers to be able to easily see a first letter or a last letter. Second, larger spaces allow enough room for a child's finger to touch under each word while reading it. Crisp pointing helps develop firm one-to-one matching, but there must be enough space for young fingers.

- Some simple sentence structures are repeated, so the child's attention can focus on directional movement and matching voice to print. As readers become comfortable with these skills, you'll ditch the patterned texts. You don't want to give children the idea that reading is about remembering repeated patterns and if you give them patterned books for too long, this is the message you send. But for a short time, when they need that support in order to focus on early print concepts, patterned books are helpful.

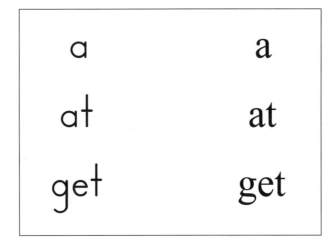

FIGURE 4.2

Notice how different these words look when you change the font. Which is the easiest for a print novice to read?

- Finally, quality books will use natural language structures and not sound contrived. We've seen too many early readers subjected to "decodable texts" at these early levels that only use words that follow a certain phonics rule and end up sounding awkward and unnatural. If you want children to just practice a phonics skill in this way, they might as well read a list of words. If you want them to learn to read books, they need practice in texts that sound like normal books and do not overemphasize a particular phonics skill.

Just a word of caution, as you pick books for your small group, you will want to avoid the following:

- Topics or names used only because of a particular phonics principle. These books can distort natural language structures and be difficult for a novice reader to understand.
- Caption books that do not allow enough practice of left-to-right movement and one-to-one matching.
- Books that lack familiar high frequency words.

It's a good idea to have particular lightbulb moments in mind to watch for as students read leveled books. Again, this will help you stay focused on big goals, rather than a scattering of skills. In Pre-A text, you looked to see if children could keep their eyes on the print and point to words with support from you. If they could do that, you knew Pre-A text had done its job. Now you'll be looking to see that your children can handle moving left to right while pointing to what they're reading in simple, patterned books. You'll be watching for them to start recognizing and writing a few high frequency words. When you see these lightbulbs go off, you'll know that Levels A and B have done their job.

TEACHING WITH LEVELS A AND B TEXTS

Now let's take a closer look at each of the lesson components we propose for working with students in this area of need (See Figure 4.3). As we describe each component, we'll keep our focus on the big goals we set for teaching with Levels A and B. It can be easy to get lost in checklists for levels that contain a myriad of skills to be learned. But too many teaching

Day 1	Day 2	Optional Day 3
Introduce and read a new book	Reread book from Lesson 1	Read familiar books
Word learning	Writing	Word learning
Letter learning	Letter learning	Letter learning

FIGURE 4.3
Text Levels A and B Lesson Cycle

points and too many new things to focus on create confused children and scattered teachers. So, at this point, keep your focus on just a few things:

- directionality, including return sweep to the left
- one-to-one matching of voice to print
- learning some anchors in print (high frequency words and letters)

Introducing the New Book

We talked in Chapter 1 about the components of a helpful book introduction. Remember you'll want to support your readers' use of various sources of information as they read. So, your introduction to the new book should feed them some information about the book topic and language structures and call their attention to print information. Let's talk more specifically now about what this can look like with Levels A and B books.

Big Idea

Begin introducing the book by giving your readers a heads up about the big, general idea of the book. Think of how you might tell a friend about a book you've just read. You'd help them categorize the book in some way—murder mystery, love story, historical fiction. Admittedly, finding a big idea in a Level A book is a stretch. How much plot can there be when every page starts with "I see. . . ."? But teachers are creative, and we know you are too. You can find a storyline in these little books, and in doing so, you are helping your children find a purpose in reading books, right from the start. Consider the Handprints Level A book, *The Fence*. The text is:

> Look at the fence.
> Look at the horse.
> Look at the cow.
> Look at the goat.
> Look at the pig.
> Look at the fence!
> Come back!

On their own, the words provide very little in the way of a storyline or a plot. But with the pictures, we see rising action unfolding. A farm fence with a small crack is chewed by a horse. A cow comes along and gives it a hip bump, causing more cracks. A goat comes along with a head butt, which topples the fence. What will the animals do now that the fence isn't holding them in? (Spoiler alert: They escape with a frantic farmer chasing behind them.)

Now think about two different approaches to providing an opening statement about the book.

> **EXAMPLE 1:** "In this book, *The Fence*, we are going to **look at** a fence and **look at** some different animals. Let's see what we will **look at**."

EXAMPLE 2: "In this book, **The Fence**, some farm animals discover something wrong with the fence that keeps them in their field. Let's see what they discover about their fence and see what they each do about it!"

Which opening do you think might lure children into story reading, rather than reading just to get the words right? Creative authors and publishers, when teamed with expert teachers, can provide early readers with authentic reading experiences.

Meaning and Language Structure

Now you and your readers will begin a short exploration of the book. Keep everyone on the same page so you can all think together about what you're seeing and thinking. You can decide if you need to call their attention to every page or if you just need to sample a few pages. You don't need to look at every page if you think there are pages that are well supported by the picture.

Meaning and language structure go hand in hand in these very early books, as almost every page has the same sentence structure. Use this structure in your language several times as you sample the pages of the books together with the children. For example, look at pages 8 to 9 of *The Fence* (see Figure 4.4).

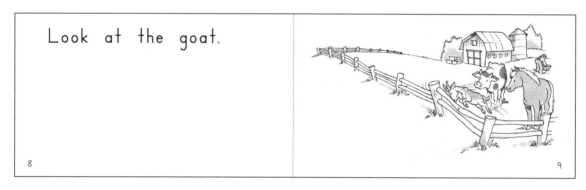

FIGURE 4.4
The Fence, *Pages 8 to 9*

"Let's turn the page to page 8 now. Who do you need to **look at** now? Yes, you're right! The goat! You need to **look at the goat** to see what he's doing to the fence."

If you can use the language structure of the book, while keeping the children's attention on the storyline at the same time, consider yourself a rock star.

As you move into some slightly harder Level B books, your readers will encounter some slight changes in pattern. At first, you'll want to include the change in language in your introduction. As the children become able to look for changes in pattern themselves, you may want to back off calling attention to it in the introduction. With their first books with pattern changes though, hearing the different words will make it easier for them to notice when they see it visually. Take a look at two pages from the Level B book *A Seed* (see Figure 4.5). In this book, the author changes the language pattern by using the word *a* on some pages and *the* on others.

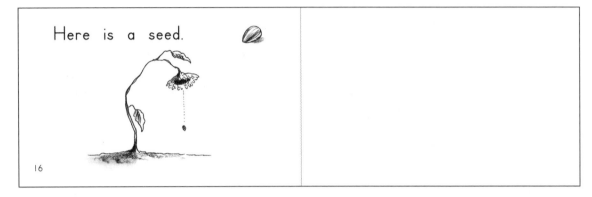

FIGURE 4.5
A Seed, *Pages 14 to 16*

A teacher might help children notice this change in pattern by using the language of the book as she introduces the book. "Let's look on page 14 and see what the boy is showing you. Wow, here is the flower! So that's what he was growing! The flower! Do you see the words *the flower*? Point to them and read them . . . *the* . . . *flower*. Good! And now turn the page to see what happens next. Yes, a seed. A seed that can start the whole process over again! Where does it say, 'a seed'? Yes, read those two words . . . *a* . . . *seed*."

By having the children locate the words in print, they will be less likely to get tripped up by the changes from *a* to *the* throughout this book. They have now added print information to their sampling of the text, so let's talk more about that.

Print Information

In general, this is the new learning for children in the early stages of literacy. Reading involves using increasing amounts of details in the print. It's tempting to try to teach children to use all those details right from the start but remember that too much scattered teaching creates confusion. Keep yourself focused on your goals.

Call attention to the print on a few pages. Over time, you'll learn to judge how many times during a book introduction you ask the children to examine the print. It may be just a couple of times, or it may be more—especially when they're learning something new. Your goal for this level is to secure left-to-right direction, one-to-one word matching, and how to anchor all this with a few known words, so those are the features you will call attention to.

CHAPTER 4

Remember that your book introduction should take just a few minutes, so don't overdo this! Here are two examples of what you might say during an introduction of *The Fence*.

> **EXAMPLE 1:** "Let's look at the words on page 8. Put your finger under the first word and take a look. Is that a word you know? Yes, it's *Look*! So, you have to say *Look* when you point to that word. Let's read this page together. Get your fingers and eyes ready. Look . . . at . . . the . . . goat. Well done! And where is the word *the*? Put your finger under *the*. Great, you know that word!"
>
> **EXAMPLE 2:** "Let's look at the words on page 8. Do you see any words that you know? Yes, Jessie found the word *Look*. Point to it and say it! Good! Does anyone see the word *the*? Great, let's point to it and say it. Now, let's read that page together. Look . . . at . . . . the . . . goat. Great reading!"

Make sure you're watching your readers during this time to see if they are pointing and looking at the right words. Intervene if needed. Reach across the table to point with a child, or direct their finger, or show them where to look. Learning about direction is best done through modeling and a guiding hand, rather than through explanations. Avoid saying things like "Go left to right and now sweep back." Just show them and guide them, saying "This way" or "Like this" as you model.

Concluding Statement

Now it's time for your children to enjoy reading their book. Give a final reminder about the big idea so it's fresh in their minds. And you may want to give a fresh reminder of the learning goal as well.

"I know we're all anxious now to read about these ornery animals and what they do to their fence. Remember to point to each word as you read."

Be quick and economical with your language. The more you talk, the less time there is to read and learn from print.

Reading the New Book

We talked about some guidelines for the reading of the new book in Chapter 1, and those guidelines will be helpful here. However, since these books will be the first that your children experience in guided reading, you may need to do a bit of modeling in order to get routines established. Your readers will each read independently at their own pace, using a whisper voice. Model this for the first couple of books, so they understand how to keep their voices soft enough to not disturb their neighbor, but loud enough for you to listen in to their reading. Also, explain that if they finish the book, they are to read it again. They should learn to keep reading on their own until you pull the group back together again.

Listen in to each child. You can go around the table in order, but as one ear listens to the one child, keep the other ear on the rest of the children, listening for anyone who is showing confusion or seems to be needing help. You'll get very good at listening to more than one child at once. Just as teachers have eyes in the back of their heads, they have ears there too!

Keep an eye out for powerful opportunities to move readers forward during and after the reading of a new book. This is the heart of guided reading. You are guiding and the children are reading. Let's talk first about the prompting and teaching you can do as children read

Levels A and B, then about the teaching points you can make at the end of the reading, and finally about the behaviors you can model now but not call for until the next band of levels.

Teaching and Prompting During Reading

In Pre-A, you explicitly modeled and practiced directional movement and pointing to words. Now your readers will try it on their own, with you supporting them when needed. You may still need to model and explain the new behaviors you expect in this new level. You will also support your readers with prompts as they read. Keep your prompts fairly short. The more language you're putting in a child's ear, the more attention and energy they have to pay to you and less they have to spend on the reading itself. Also, children will take on your language to guide themselves. It's easier for them to do this if your language is simple and quick.

Let's look at some prompts and teaching moves that will be very helpful in supporting directional movement, one-to-one matching, and noticing some familiar words (see Figure 4.6). Prompting and supporting follows a continuum from most to least supportive and a general guideline is to use the least supportive prompt you can, in order to give the most independence to the learner. For instance, if a child reads more words than are on the page you might say, "Were you right?" If the child continues to mismatch you might try the prompt, "That didn't match. Try that again." If the child still can't fix the mismatch say, "Let's read it together. You point under the words and I'll point above the words and we'll make it match."

Directional Movement

For many children, directional movement comes naturally and quickly. Other children will need lots of guided practice to internalize automatically moving their eyes across print in that way. Talking about direction to children can also be very confusing. For this behavior, the fewer words the better. A lot less talk and a lot more action is the best motto for directional behavior. Here are some ideas to help teach this.

- Prompt with a few words, but mostly demonstrate. For example, "Start here." Demonstrate. "Go this way." Demonstrate.
- Give readers a visual reminder of where to start. Some teachers place a small green dot at the starting point for reading and writing.
- Make sure students do a lot of writing. Writing gives constant practice in left-to-right behavior.

Matching Voice to Print

For some children, it is a real challenge to slow their speech down enough to hear individual words, and then match the oral words to printed words by noticing the spaces in the text. It's a lot to juggle simultaneously. For these children, you may need some very precise, explicit teaching.

- Prompting:
  "Point under the word so your eyes can see it."
  "I'll point above the word and you point below. Let's read it together."
  "Make it match. You ran out of words."
  "Slow down and check each word."

	Directional Movement	One-to-one Matching	Noticing Familiar Words
New behavior	- "Do it like this." (model) - "This way." (model)	- "Point *under* the word so your eyes can see it." - "I'll point above the word and you point below. Let's read it together." - Have the child two-finger frame each word. - Have the child point with the eraser end of a pencil. - Cut up a sentence from the book and have the child put the words in order with very exaggerated spaces between words. Point and read.	- Use the book to teach high frequency words. Read a page together, locate the target word, then teach the word.
Inconsistent behavior	- Tap or gently move child's finger in the correct direction.	- "Did it match? Check to make sure." - "Did you have enough words? Too many words?"	- "The word *see* is on this page. Can you find it? Run your finger under it and read it." - "Now find *see* on another page in this book."
Almost secure behavior	- "Yay! You started in the right place and went the right way."	- Praise - "You really made it match." - "When it didn't match, you fixed it."	- "What words do you see that you know on this page?" - Mask all the text except the target word. "Is this a word you know? What is it?"

FIGURE 4.6
Summary Table of Teaching with Levels A and B

- Use hands-on props if needed—but be cautious. Get rid of the manipulative as soon as possible. Props distract attention from the act of reading and create a crutch that can hinder progress. But for your children who need it, here are a few ideas:
  - Cut up a sentence from the book and have the child put the words in order with very exaggerated spaces between words. Point and read.
  - Have the child point with the eraser end of a pencil. Avoid using cute witch fingers or other gimmicky pointers. These attract children's eyes to the witch finger, rather than the words. (Sorry! We know how cute they are!)
  - Have the child use both index fingers to frame each word. Once they can do this, however, quickly transition to finger pointing below the word.

Noticing Familiar Words

Remember that the main behaviors we want to establish at this point are directional movement and one-to-one matching. The next helpful behaviors will involve monitoring words when the text is not patterned. But, of course, to do this, children need to know some words. So, while children are working on learning the rules of the road, they will be simultaneously learning some helpful high frequency words in the Word Learning component of the lesson. During text reading, you can support this learning by calling attention to the words. However, note this important distinction. Here, we're asking them to just notice the words, in preparation for the future when they really have to use the words.

You may want to keep magnetic letters handy. If a child finishes reading a book, you can quickly hand the letters for a target word and ask him to find the word and make it. You can also keep whiteboards near each child and ask them to quickly write a word when they finish the book.

Teaching Points After the Reading

When all your readers have read the new book at least one time through, you'll want to pull everyone back together. This will be a chance for two things—enjoying the content of the book and reiterating a teaching point that you want them to remember.

First, always first, say something about the content of the book. Have a little conversation. It could be about the plot, the character, what was funny, what was surprising, a connection they have, or anything that comes to mind about the book. A reader's main focus should be the story so talk about that first!

Then, state a clear point about reading that you want them to remember. In this case, it's likely going to be about how you saw them all pointing and matching their spoken words to printed words. Or you might mention that every time they pointed to the word *see*, they said the word *see*. You don't need to belabor it, but by succinctly stating what you expect from their reading, you're more likely to see children take on those behaviors.

Rereading Familiar Books

In our lesson cycles, Lesson 2 and Lesson 3 involve reading previously read books. Lesson 2's book will always be the previous lesson's new book. Lesson 3 can be any books that were previously read. The children love reading familiar books for several reasons. They are usually

CHAPTER 4

very successful because it's now familiar. In Lesson 3, there can be choice involved if you put out several familiar books and let them pick and choose what they read. And children love returning to familiar characters and stories to enjoy them again and again. As the teacher, you may love this component because you get a chance to take observational notes, take a running record, or work intensively with one student if you see a need. Plus, since this is more of an in-the-moment, responsive interaction, you don't have to plan this component! Yay! If you use this time well, you may find it to be one of the most valuable for teaching and learning.

Learning Words

Readers are now beginning the never-ending task of adding words to their reading and writing vocabularies. Recognizing some words automatically eases the burden of needing to solve every word, increases fluency, and gives the reader a sampling of various phonics patterns from which to build new words. The words that are most helpful in Levels A and B are the high frequency words found in the particular books you use. In general, a nice compromise can be found in teaching words from your guided reading books and teaching district-mandated words, which often come from the Fry Sight Word list or the Dolch list. There is usually plenty of overlap. The primary purpose of learning high frequency words at this level, however, is to have footholds in print. These words act as anchors for the eyes and give the reader something to monitor to determine if they are reading correctly. You'll most certainly want to teach the high frequency words that appear most often in your guided reading books.

Since this word-learning journey never ends, the most important thing for children to learn at this point is *how* to learn new words. They need a system for studying words in an efficient way and committing them to memory. This system should make use of letters, sounds, and word parts they will have to remember. This is all part of a process called *orthographic mapping* (Ehri 2013), which also includes learning spelling, pronunciation, and the meaning of words. Just keep in mind the principles we discussed in Chapter 1 and try to involve seeing, hearing, saying, and moving to help children learn. Mapping the sounds they hear to the letters they see will help anchor words in their brain. Committing words to long-term memory takes more than one experience with them, so plan to return to words in subsequent lessons. Let's take a look at what learning a word might look like (see Figure 4.7).

Materials

- teacher whiteboard or chart paper, dark marker
- magnetic letters
- baggies for personal collection of magnetic letters and word cards
- whiteboards for each child, dry erase markers, erasers or socks for erasing
- index cards or tagboard cards

Procedures for Learning a New Word

After reading books is the perfect time to learn a new word. This can be done right after reading a new book or a familiar book. Take your children back to a page in the book that

FIGURE 4.7
*Learning Words Materials. Notice the variety of hands
on materials you can use to teach high frequency words.*

uses the target word. Read a sentence that contains the word, take a close look at it, and then work on learning it.

1. Read a sentence from a book with the target word.
2. Write the word in large letters on a whiteboard or chart while the children watch. Say it as you write it. Point out the parts of the words with letter sounds they know and can match.
3. Distribute baggies of magnetic letters with the letters for each child to make the word. They should make it, then run their finger under it as they read it and check it with their eyes. Then mix the letters up and make it again several times.
4. Leave the book open in front of them so they can reread the page with the word as they work.
5. Return to this word in subsequent lessons. You can have children repeat making the words with magnetic letters or have them write the word several times on whiteboards. Make sure they say the word and check it with their eyes and finger every time they write it.

6. When you feel the word is pretty well known, make a word card for each child to add to their baggie of known words. This collection of words can be used to practice speeded recognition of their words or as a quick check to see which words they are remembering. We caution you not to introduce too many new words at one time or move a word to a word card if children are giving wild guesses when they see it in print.

To get a feel for how this might sound in a lesson, see Mrs. Jones's example lesson (Figure 4.13) at the end of the chapter.

Procedures for Practicing Known and Partially Known Words

Committing a word to long-term memory takes more than one experience with it, so plan to return to words in subsequent lessons. It's tempting to think that once we've taught a word and witnessed a child reading or writing it correctly, it's "known." Resist thinking this! Rather than categorizing items as "known" or "not known" consider how well they are known along a continuum. Think back to when you (or your teenage child) first got your driver's license. Sure, you passed the test. You "knew" how to drive. But could you drive well in adverse conditions? Could you make instant quality decisions? Could you multitask safely? That level of knowing probably took years. It won't take years for our children to learn a new word, but they will need to experience the word in a variety of contexts and in unexpected places to recognize it instantly every time. To help retain words in long-term memory and get faster and faster at recognizing them, we use a few different activities.

- Once children have a large enough set of word cards, occasionally have them sort their words into two piles: *I Know These Words* and *I Don't Know These Words Yet*. Have each child read their pile of known words and then have them pick one word to practice on their whiteboard. This goes pretty quickly because at this level, they don't have too many cards. Sorting into these two piles is valuable for both the child and you. The child must search their brain for what they know and don't know. They also get a sense for which words they want to learn next. Sometimes when children are given the task of reading word cards, they make a guess at every card because they think they are supposed to. This is very unhelpful because it can code an incorrect response in their brain. By telling them to figure out which ones they don't know, they understand that it's okay not to know them all yet. And as the teacher, you get a quick sense of who knows what—a nice formative assessment.
- Give each child an array of magnetic letters that can be used to make several known words. Prompt them: "What words can you make? Show me. Now try *see*. Now try *is*." Starting with the prompt "What words can you make?" is again helpful to both the child and you. The child benefits by searching their brain for what they know. They may see an *s* and begin searching their brain for words that start with *s*. As the teacher, you get a window into what your readers know quickly and automatically with no prompting. Again, you get a quick formative assessment from a learning activity.
- Give each child a whiteboard and prompt them to write any words they remember that they've practiced. Emphasize that it should be a word they've practiced, or this activity can morph into an invented spelling activity—which is valuable but not the point here. The same rationale applies here. The children are searching their brains and practicing words to make them more automatically known. You are watching the process to know what you might need to teach.

Writing

When working in text levels A and B, writing moves from the shared pen work in Pre-A to everyone having the opportunity to write the entire "story" with support. Remember, writing during the small group looks different than the writing that takes place throughout the rest of the day. Here, you need to be in control of the writing content, so you can maximize each child's learning. You need to be constantly thinking what you want your children to learn next in reading, so you can reciprocate that learning through writing. Carefully constructed "stories" provide opportunities to work on phonemic awareness, phonics skills, letter learning, word learning, concepts of print, and, of course, reading.

Materials

Prior to beginning your lessons in text Levels A and B, you will want to do some prep work by gathering (see Figure 4.8):

- a white board to model the writing
- a highlighter marker
- a writing booklet for each child
- a writing utensil for each student; dark markers contrast well against a white piece of paper
- white correction tape

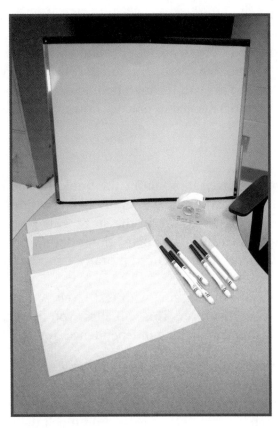

FIGURE 4.8
Writing Materials

Before Writing

Let's get back to the idea of crafting the "story." It's always easiest to craft a story from a common experience because it helps increase student engagement. For your group, the common experience will be the new book introduced in the first lesson. Even though you will preplan what the group will write, you should lead a conversation about the book before you dictate the story, to connect the experience to reading and meaning. In most instances, your discussion will bring up what you have planned to write.

As you plan your story, you will want to ask yourself these questions:

- What language from the book would be good to use?
- What word or words will my children be able to write fast?
- What high frequency word do my children need to learn?
- What word would lend itself well to analysis with sound boxes?
- What letters do my children need to learn or practice?

The chart in Figure 4.9 highlights Mrs. Jones's thinking as she answers these questions for her writing time with Johnny, Aubrey, E.J., and Karie. Notice how, in some cases, there may be several answers to each question. Her goal is to look at her lesson notes and assessments to determine what she will teach during writing. For example, when her group read *The Cave* she knew from her notes:

1. All four children could read and write the words *the, is,* and *a* fast and fluently, with little mental energy spent on the task.
2. *Rat* would be a good word to analyze in sound boxes because the children would be able to easily hear a beginning consonant, middle vowel, and ending consonant.
3. The children needed to learn the high frequency word *look.*
4. Several of the children needed to practice how to write the letter s.

During Writing

After having a brief conversation about the book, dictate the story to your children. It's important that they practice saying it orally before writing it. You might even count, on your fingers, how many words are in the story. This practice helps each child to get the story language into their head and helps them develop listening for whole words in our language. Once students have practiced it orally, hand out the materials they need to write the story.

In the early lessons of engaging with text levels A and B, it is often easier to have the group stay together as they write. This will allow you to teach the procedures and gradually release children as they gain writing independence. You will want to make sure:

- **You model the writing.** Writing with them provides visual supports many children need as they begin their journeys to becoming writers.
- **Students begin in the top left corner of the page.** You can touch each child's page to show them where to start or have each child touch the page where they will start. If you have the children show where to start, you can quickly correct those that try to begin on the right or at the bottom of the page.

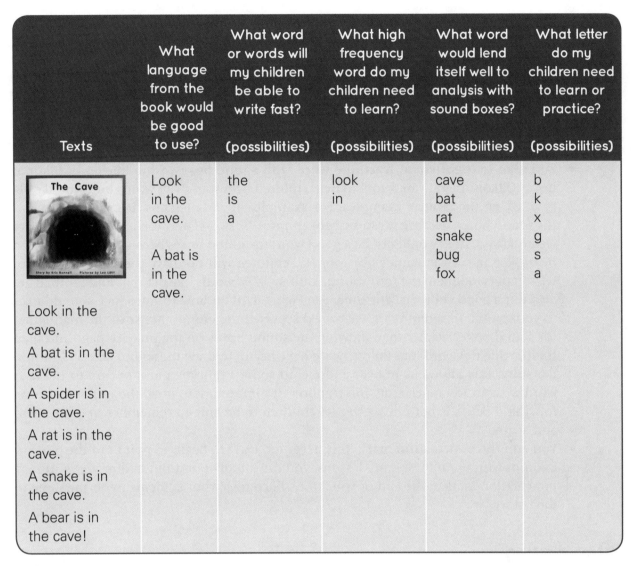

Texts	What language from the book would be good to use?	What word or words will my children be able to write fast? (possibilities)	What high frequency word do my children need to learn? (possibilities)	What word would lend itself well to analysis with sound boxes? (possibilities)	What letter do my children need to learn or practice? (possibilities)
The Cave — Look in the cave. A bat is in the cave. A spider is in the cave. A rat is in the cave. A snake is in the cave. A bear is in the cave!	Look in the cave. A bat is in the cave.	the is a	look in	cave bat rat snake bug fox	b k x g s a

FIGURE 4.9
Teaching Opportunities During Writing

- **Students manage the space on the page.** Some children, in their early writing careers, can manage the space on the paper well and others cannot. They write their letters too large and place them anywhere on the page. For these children, you can scaffold their learning by using your highlighter and give one horizontal line for each word in the story. The length of the line should be approximately the length of the word. For example, *is* would need a short line and *motorcycle* would need a long line. This scaffold is usually only needed until students take on the task of managing the space themselves.
- **Students chorally say the story and write the first word.** It is helpful in your planning to make sure you start your story with a known word. This builds confidence and gets the writing off to a good start.
- **Students reread after each new word is written in the story.** Rereading gives your students the opportunity to practice correct left-to right-directionality and one-to-one voice-to-print matching, and helps with remembering what word comes next in the story.

- **You encourage fast responding.** Students should be expected or prompted to write known letters and words fast. You might say, "Oh! We know the word *the*! Remember, when we know a word, we write it fast!"

- **You keep to one or possibly two new high frequency words to practice.** Choose your words carefully, thinking about what will pop up again and again in the next books your children will read. During the lesson, take the time to have children run through the word on their practice page three to four times, before adding it quickly to their story.

- **You plan to highlight at least one word with sound boxes.** Sound boxes or Elkonin boxes (Elkonin 1971) are a tool to help children hear sounds in words but should only be used on the clearest examples. For example, in early lessons, *bus* is a good word for sound boxes because it can be broken into /b/ /u/ /s/ and each sound can be very clearly heard. *Book* would not be a good word for sound boxes because, although it can be broken into clear sounds, /b/ /oo/ /k/, children will not have the experience yet of what letters to link to the /oo/ sound. Multisyllabic words like octopus and football are also not a good choice at this time. See Figure 4.10 on how to introduce sound boxes to your group. In recent years, we have discovered the important use of the highlighter for sound boxes. Rather than drawing the sound boxes on the practice page and then transferring the word into the story, we have begun to draw the sound boxes right into the story. This allows us to hear and record sounds quickly and move on to the next word without too much story interruption. It's important to note, the word we choose for sound boxes is not one we expect children to be able to remember to write again and again.

- **You add the punctuation mark.** It is never too early to begin to point out the punctuation in writing. In these early lessons, you can simply point out and model putting a punctuation mark at the end of your story. Encourage your students to do the same in their story.

After Writing

Once they're finished writing, it is important for all the children to read the story one final time in its entirety. As they read, watch for correct left-to-right directionality and one-to-one voice-to-print matching. Be ready to intervene if a student is not being precise with their pointing. If time allows, students always enjoy drawing a quick sketch of the story. The sketch will help them remember what they wrote when they come back to read their story later.

Learning Letters

Once again, we end our small group lessons working with letters. Most likely, there will still be letters your children need to learn as they move into working with text levels A and B. Just a reminder from Chapter 3: You will need to continue to explicitly *teach* unknown letters and children will need to *practice* partially known and known letters to build automaticity.

Introducing Sound Boxes

Initially, sound boxes should be introduced as a phonemic activity. You will want your children to gain control of the coordination of eyes, voice, and finger before adding letters. To get started you will need simple picture cards that represent words that are comprised of two, three, or four sounds and sound boxes with two, three, or four boxes.

Here are some of examples of words matched with the appropriate sound boxes:

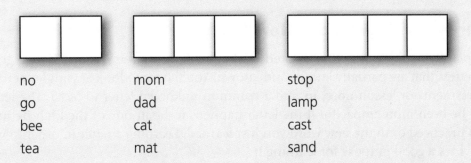

no	mom	stop
go	dad	lamp
bee	cat	cast
tea	mat	sand

Coordinating the use of sound boxes is the most difficult task. You should be meticulous in teaching it and then calling for it from your children. Here are the steps:

1. Say the word slowly.
2. Say the word slowly again and touch one box, from left to right, for each sound in the word.
3. Say the word fast.

Once your children are able to coordinate the eyes, voice, and finger, you can add the letters in the boxes as you go. Here are the steps:

1. Say the word slowly.
2. Say the word slowly again and touch one box, from left to right, for each sound in the word.
3. Say the word again, stopping your voice and finger on the first box.
4. Link the letter to the sound you are producing.
5. Write the letter in the box.
6. Say the word again, touch the boxes, and stop your voice and finger on the second box.
7. Link the letter to the sound you are producing.
8. Write the letter in the second box.
9. Do the same for boxes three and four.
10. Point and read the whole word.

CHAPTER 4

FIGURE 4.10
How to Introduce Sound Boxes

Materials

The materials you gathered for Pre-A lessons will continue to be useful when working with text levels A and B (see Chapter 3, Learning Letters, page 37). We also encourage you to add a set of **letter cards**, upper case and lower case, for each child. You will want to choose or make a set of cards that uses a simple font. We tend to choose a font that closely matches the ones we see in the books we use for small groups. These simple fonts help children to distinguish the features of each letter more easily.

Procedures for Teaching a New Letter

Hopefully by this point, the children working with text levels A and B have a good number of letters that are partially known and known. You'll have to look at your letter identification assessments or lesson notes to find a common unknown letter to *teach*. The letter learning can be even more impactful if the letter happens to be in one of the high frequency words you practiced or in the new word you just learned. Learning a letter in order to write a word provides a good purpose for learning it.

The procedures for learning a new letter do not change from Chapter 3 (see Chapter 3, Letter Learning, page 39). Just remember, a child is more likely to remember a letter if all areas of their brain are activated. When you introduce the new letter, be sure children do the following:

- **see it** in a word and in their ABC book
- **hear** the name of the letter
- **verbalize** the letter formation
- **feel** the way to write it
- **say** the name of the letter

Procedures for Practicing Partially Known and Known Letters

Remember from Chapter 1, each time a child practices a partially known letter, connections between neurons in the brain grow stronger. By making those connections stronger, children build automaticity, meaning you can begin to call for faster, more fluent responding to the twenty-five or more letters they partially know or know. Again, you can continue to choose from the procedures in Chapter 3 (Procedures for Teaching a New Letter, see page 40). The following are some additional options we start to include in our lessons about this time.

- Using their own baggie of partially known and known letters, each child should line the letters up into a letter array. This can be done on a magnetic tray or just on the tabletop. Once a child has built the letter array, they should push each letter up and name it quickly from left to right. They should repeat the process again, only this time they should pull the letters down as they name them.
- Letter sorting creates opportunities for children to look closely at the attributes of letters and distinguish one letter from another. You can offer magnetic letters, letter tiles, letter cards, and letter stamps as materials to sort. Once a child has sorted their set of letters, they should name the letters in each category fast. Here are some categories to sort letters by but certainly not all of the possibilities:
    - capital letters and lower-case letters
    - colors

- curves/no curves
- lines/no lines
- curves or lines/curves and lines
- tall/short
- circles/sticks
- let your children decide how to sort the group of letters
- My Pile/Your Pile (Clay 2005b)is the game you need the letter cards to play. You want children to feel successful, so you need to be thoughtful about what letters to include in the game. You will definitely want the known letters and partially known letters along with three to five letters a child still needs to learn. Once a child knows thirty letters or more, you can use all fifty-two letters when you play the game.
    - Initially, this game is played one on one with each child. Shuffle up the letters and show them one at a time. If they can name it fast, it goes in "your pile" (child's pile). If the child can't name the letter or is too slow, the letter goes in "my pile" (teacher's pile). After going through all the letter cards, encourage them to name the letters in their pile again FAST. Tuck the pile of letters you collected away for another day.
    - While you are playing the game with one child, the rest of the children practice naming the pile of letters they collected FAST, several times if time allows.
    - Occasionally, you will want to shuffle all fifty-two cards back together, play the game again with each child and re-sort their cards. This is a very visual way for a child to see their learning taking place because their pile will be growing larger than your pile over time. Once children are consistently naming the uppercase letters fast, you can pull those twenty-six letters out and only use the lower-case letter cards until those have been mastered too.

FIGURE 4.11A
Letters that Have Lines *or* No Lines

FIGURE 4.11B
Letters that Have Circles *or* No Circles

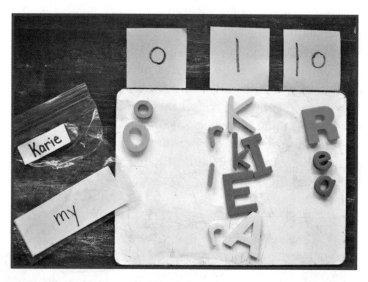

FIGURE 4.11C
Letters that Have Circles *or* Lines *or* Both a Circle and a Line

Remember to check out our correlating literacy center ideas that support the work students are doing at the small group table with text Levels A and B.

www.stenhouse.com/content/intentional-from-the-start

REMEMBER THE PURPOSE OF TEACHING WITH LEVELS A AND B TEXTS

Learning the rules of the road takes time and experience, whether you're a driver or a reader. The first thing a new driver learns is to stay on the correct side of the road. Knowing which way to head down the street needs to be automatic, with little conscious attention, because drivers have lots of other decisions to make as they drive. If you've ever driven in England, you know how rapidly your driving skills deteriorate when you're so consciously focused on going the right direction down the street. As you learn the meanings of a few street signs, you can use those to make sure you are staying on track. Reading is similar. Directional movement and one-to-one matching need to go on autopilot and it's hard for that to happen when the brain is working on too many challenges. Books in levels A and B give your readers the supportive experience they need to become automatic in early reading behaviors without too many other decisions to make. The high frequency words they learn at this time are another way for them to check on themselves and stay on track. Once these early behaviors are secure, readers will have more brainpower available to take on other reading challenges.

As your readers head into harder Level B and Level C books, they are going to be called on to monitor high frequency words, self-correct errors, and solve new words. Big challenges! So just as brave driver's ed teachers work to ensure their students' directional skills are firmly in place before heading out to the highway, take time in these levels to make sure your young readers know the rules of the road.

EXAMPLE LESSON WITH LEVEL A TEXT

Mrs. Jones has chosen the book *Traffic Jam* (Figure 4.12) for her children to read. It is a topic most children will have experienced at one time or another in the car with their parents. She knows from her lesson records that all four children know the words *I* and *a* so she selected this book knowing they'll have anchor words for their eyes to gravitate to. She will teach *see* as the new high frequency word and plans to have students practice the letter *s* because Johnny still calls it a *c*, it is the first letter in the word *see,* and it can be a tricky letter to form. Let's listen in as Mrs. Jones guides her small group through a lesson using the Level A text *Traffic Jam* (Figure 4.13).

FIGURE 4.12
Traffic Jam, *Cover*

Component: Introduce and Read a New Text: Traffic Jam
Focuses: Look at print; left to right directionality; one-to-one voice-to-print matching

Mrs. Jones gathers E.J., Karie, Aubrey, and Johnny at the small group table to read the book *The Traffic Jam*. She plans to have the children read the book, learn the new word *see*, and practice how to form the letter *s* correctly. Mrs. Jones starts the conversation by learning more about the children's background knowledge about a traffic jam. This helps her know how much information to provide in order to support their successful reading.

Student and Teacher Interactions	Teacher Moves and Rationale
Mrs. Jones: This book called *The Traffic Jam* is all about the kinds of vehicles you might see in a traffic jam. Let's take a quick look at a few pictures.	Mrs. Jones decides to show the pages with a bus, firetruck, and van because they might be tricky for the children when they come to them.
Mrs. Jones (showing the firetruck): Hmmmm. What vehicle do you see on this page? **E.J.:** A fire engine! **Aubrey:** A firetruck! **Mrs. Jones:** Well both of you are right. This vehicle can be called a fire engine or a firetruck. The author of this book decided to call it a firetruck. Let's clap the word *firetruck*. **Group** (clapping): fire-truck	Mrs. Jones shows the firetruck because she knows most children call it either a fire engine or firetruck. She wants to have the children focus on how long the word is.
Mrs. Jones: Great job clapping! *Firetruck* is a long word; it has two claps. (Pointing to the word *firetruck*.) Look how long the word is and watch me point to it as I say it . . . fiiiiiirrrrrretrrrrrruuuuck. Read the page with me while I point to the words: I see a firetruck.	As the children read the page, Mrs. Jones is precise with her one-to-one voice-to-print matching. Mrs. Jones goes to the page with the van next because the picture is tricky. She knows the children cannot rely on the picture for assistance because the *van* looks more like a small *bus*. So, she decides to read the page, modeling one-to-one voice-to-print matching and voicing the initial sound in *van*.

FIGURE 4.13
Example Lesson for The Traffic Jam

	This allows the children to think about what would make sense and give possibilities. Once they come to a consensus that it could be *van*, she models looking at the word closely to see if the letters match the sounds in *van*.
Mrs. Jones: Now it's time for you to read the book *Traffic Jam*. Read quietly and be sure to point to the words as you read. Remember, you can check the picture if you get stuck.	Mrs. Jones hands out one book to each child and they begin reading. She leans into each student individually, so she can see how the reading is going and how she can prompt and teach. She leans into Johnny first.
Johnny (Looks at the bus and reads the picture without looking at the words): I see a bus. **Mrs. Jones**: Johnny, I noticed your eyes were looking at the picture as you read that page. Read it again, and this time make sure your eyes look at the words while you point. **Johnny:** (Attends to the words this time and points) I see a bus. **Mrs. Jones:** That time your eyes looked at the words and you pointed to every word your mouth said! Keep doing that good reading work!	Mrs. Jones is careful to watch each child's eyes as she leans in to listen to them read. She knows they may glance at the picture before reading the page. They may even quickly glance from the print to the picture and back to the print. But the main goal is for the students' eyes to be mostly looking at the print.
Karie (with precise pointing): I see a . . . what's that word? **Mrs. Jones:** Check the picture, what vehicle do you see? **Karie:** A car. **Mrs. Jones:** Right! Now read the words since the picture helped you to figure that out! **Karie:** I see a car!	Mrs. Jones listens to Karie next. When she gets stuck on a word, Mrs. Jones decides in the moment how to help her become a strategic reader. In this instance she decides to direct Karie to check the picture to help solve the word she is stuck on.

FIGURE 4.13   (*Continued*)

E.J.: I see a (looks at the picture)—I don't know what that is Mrs. Jones.
Mrs. Jones: I see a /j/, /j/, /j/ . . .
E.J.: Jeep! (Slides his finger under the sentence rather than matching his voice to print) I see a jeep.
Mrs. Jones: E.J., try that again and this time point to each word as you read.
E.J.: (With more precise pointing) I see a jeep.
Mrs. Jones: Great pointing! I noticed your eyes were looking at the words.

Mrs. Jones leans into E.J. next.
Mrs. Jones decides to produce the first letter sound in the word *jeep*. It is just enough information for E.J. to think about what would make sense here. Since Mrs. Jones's goal is to make sure directionality and voice-to-print matching are under control she chooses not to require E.J. to focus on and produce the first sound himself.
Whenever Mrs. Jones notices a child sliding their finger instead of matching voice to print, she encourages them to try it again and point to each word. If they are not able to match voice to print, she models for them and has them try again.

Mrs. Jones: Aubrey what's going on?
Aubrey: I finished the book.
Mrs. Jones: Great! Read it again so I can hear the great reading work you do.
Aubrey: OK (slightly annoyed). I see a bus. I see a truck. I see . . .
Mrs. Jones: Aubrey, stop for a moment. I noticed on the last two pages you stopped pointing and looking at the words. Readers must look at the words. Start on this page again, point to each word as you read and finish the book.
Aubrey: I see a firetruck. I see a jeep.
Mrs. Jones (whispers): Now you're looking! Keep going!
(The children all finish up their reading.)

Mrs. Jones turns to Aubrey who is sitting at the table with her book closed.

Mrs. Jones notes that Aubrey uses precise pointing at the beginning of the book then begins turning the pages and just looking at the picture and reciting the pattern. She decides to stop her and have her try the last few pages again.
When Aubrey returns to the text, she is much more precise at voice-to-print matching.

Mrs. Jones: I watched your eyes very carefully while you were reading. I noticed that sometimes they looked at the words. But sometimes, your eyes looked at the pictures and not the words while your mouth said the words. When you read your eyes have to look at the words. Your finger helps you by showing your eyes where to look.

Once the children have read the book a time or two, Mrs. Jones leads a brief comprehension discussion. She quickly looks at her notes to decide on the teaching point. She notices that most children had difficulty at one point or another with looking at the print and with one-to-one voice-to-print matching. She decides this is what she will reteach, model, and have the children practice.

FIGURE 4.13   *(Continued)*

CHAPTER 4

DAY 1 (Continued)

Mrs. Jones: Watch me as I point and read this page. (Mrs. Jones is very precise as she models pointing and reading.) I see a jeep. Now, it's your turn. Find your favorite page. (Mrs. Jones waits for everyone to find it.) Now look, point, and read your favorite page.

Mrs. Jones: Everyone looked at the words and pointed! That's what readers do!

Mrs. Jones carefully watches while everyone reads. Everyone is successful with looking at the print and pointing.

Component: Word Learning
Focus: Learning High Frequency Words

Mrs. Jones plans to teach the high frequency word *see* not only because it is in *The Traffic Jam* but because it will be in other books they will read in the future. Prior to the lesson, Mrs. Jones got magnetic boards and magnetic letters ready so each child can build the word *see*.

Student and Teacher Interactions

Mrs. Jones: There was a word in this book that will help us as readers and as writers. It's the word *see*. The letters in the word *see* are *s . . . e . . . e*. (Mrs. Jones builds the word on her magnetic board.) Read the word *see* as I point to it:

Group: *See.*

Mrs. Jones: You can hear the /s/ at the beginning of the word *see* and sometimes the letter *e* says /ee/. So, this word looks just the way it sounds. Read it slowly with me again and look and listen for those sounds.

Group: /sssss/ /eeeee/.

Teacher Moves and Rationale

Mrs. Jones: Now you get to make the word *see*. What is the first letter?

Group: *s!*

Mrs. Jones: Right! Here is the letter *s*. (Mrs. Jones hands a letter *s* to each child.) The next letter is *e*. Here is the letter *e*. (Mrs. Jones hands everyone the letter *e*.) The last letter in the word *see* is *e* too. Here's another *e*.

Mrs. Jones hands out the letters one at a time for the word *see*. This ensures the children grab the correct letter first and that they assemble it correctly from left to right.

FIGURE 4.13   *(Continued)*

Mrs. Jones: Put your finger under the first letter of the word. Now read that word using your finger and your eyes.
Group: *see!*
Mrs. Jones: Take a good look at that word *see* because I am going to mix it up and you are going to build it again.

Mrs. Jones quickly scans to make sure everyone has their finger under the letter *s*. She moves a child's finger if they are not pointing under the first letter *s*.

Mrs. Jones has the children build the new word three or four more times. Each time a child makes the word *see*, Mrs. Jones has them point with their finger and read it with their eyes in a left-to-right direction across the word.

Mrs. Jones: Do you think you can write the word *see* now?
Group: Yes!
Mrs. Jones: I think you can too. Try it on your board right now. I wonder, what letter will you write first?
Group: *s!*
(All the children write the word *see* on their boards.)

Mrs. Jones now has the children write the word several times, because writing the word *see* builds another neural pathway in the brain for learning the word.

For this first attempt, Mrs. Jones leaves the magnetic word *see* on each of their boards. This provides a scaffold for anyone who can't remember the order of the letters.

After building the word *see* with the support of the magnetic letters, Mrs. Jones takes them away. Mrs. Jones knows taking the magnetic word *see* away will force the children to think about what the word looks like before they write it. After each child writes the word, Mrs. Jones has them check it using their finger and their eyes before she erases it. Each child writes the word *see* three or four times.

Mrs. Jones finishes by pulling the children back into the text and finding the word *see*. She wants them to notice the words they learn will pop up often in their reading and writing work.

Component: Letter Learning
Focus: Learn new letter names and sounds; build automaticity with partially known and known letters and sounds

Mrs. Jones had prepared to teach how to write the letter *s* prior to the lesson. While students practiced writing the word *see* she noticed Johnny was still having difficulty and Karie wrote it backward so she continues with this plan.

FIGURE 4.13 *(Continued)*

	Student and Teacher Interactions	Teacher Moves and Rationale
DAY 1 (Continued)	**Mrs. Jones:** I noticed some of you had a little bit of trouble writing that curvy letter *s* in the word *see*! (Mrs. Jones points to the magnetic letter *s* in the word *see*.) So, let's practice it so we can become *s* writing experts!	
	Mrs. Jones: Start at the top, curve, slant, curve, *s*. Watch me again, *start at the top, curve, slant, curve, s*. Now let's do it in the air with our finger pencil. Be sure to make it big and say the words with me too. (All the children and Mrs. Jones say and make the letter in the air.) **Mrs. Jones:** What letter did we write? **Group**: *s*!	Mrs. Jones models how to write the letter *s* on her white board using letter formation language. Providing children the opportunity to "see, say, and do" makes their neural pathways stronger. Mrs. Jones hands out the ABC books, already turned to the letter *Ss* page. She has the children quickly trace the letters *Ss* using the letter formation language and then name them.
	Mrs. Jones: Now, write the letter *s* on your white board using the words to guide you and don't forget to name the letter too. (All the children practice saying and writing the letter *s* on their white boards.) **Mrs. Jones:** Nice job readers and writers! You read a new book and learned a new word and practiced a tricky letter today. Tomorrow we will read this book again and write about it.	While the children practice writing the letter *s*, Mrs. Jones helps those children who begin their letter backward or revert to starting at the bottom of the letter.

FIGURE 4.13   (*Continued*)

CHAPTER 4

DAY 2

Component: Reread Book from Day 1: *The Traffic Jam*
Focus: Look at print; left-to-right directionality; one-to-one voice-to-print matching

Mrs. Jones hands out *The Traffic Jam* and once again listens in to each child read a few pages. She watches carefully for one-to-one voice-to-print matching. If she notices a mismatch she decides in the moment how to prompt:

- Did that match? (Least support)
- Try that again and make it match. (More support)
- Watch me, now you try it. (Most support)

Student and Teacher Interactions	Teacher Moves and Rationale
Mrs. Jones: Yesterday, you read the book *The Traffic Jam*. Today you are going to reread it. As you read, I am going to be watching carefully to make sure you are pointing to the words your mouth is saying. Be sure to make it match. **Johnny:** (Slides his finger under the words as he reads.) I see a car . . . I see a motorcycle . . . **Mrs. Jones:** Johnny, watch me read that page. I am going to point to each word as I read it. I see a motorcycle. Now you read it. **Johnny:** I see a motorcycle. I see a firetruck. I see a jeep. **Mrs. Jones:** Now you're matching! Keep reading!	Aubrey is off to a great start with precise one-to-one voice-to-print matching so Mrs. Jones complements her and turns her attention to Johnny. Mrs. Jones notices that Johnny continues to struggle with one-to-one voice-to-print matching. She decides to model the reading behavior and have Johnny try it again. She watches him read a few more pages to make sure he continues to match.
E.J.: I see a firetruck. (He taps the page beyond the word *firetruck* for the truck part.) **Mrs. Jones:** Did that match? **E.J.:** Nope. **Mrs. Jones:** Then try it again and make it match. Remember, firetruck is a long word. **E.J.:** I see a firetruck. (This time he matches voice to print.)	When E.J. runs out of words, Mrs. Jones simply prompts him to try it again. Mrs. Jones is sure to allow enough time for each student to read the entire book two to three times while she monitors their reading.

FIGURE 4.13   (*Continued*)

Component: Writing
Focus: Start at the top left; left-to-right directionality; leaving spaces between words; writing high frequency words fast.

Prior to the lesson, Mrs. Jones decides to have the group write: *I see a bus.* This sentence will give the children an opportunity to:

- begin with a word they know.
- write *I* and *a* fast.
- practice the new high frequency word *see*.
- practice the letter *s* two times.
- solve the word *bus* in sound boxes.

If there is time the group will also write: *I see a jeep.*

Student and Teacher Interactions	Teacher Moves and Rationale
Mrs. Jones: Today we are going to write: *I see a bus.* Say the sentence with me and use your fingers to count how many words we will write. **Group:** I see a bus. (Mrs. Jones and the children hold up one finger for each word.) **Mrs. Jones:** How many words are we going to write? **Group:** Four!	Mrs. Jones leads the group in a brief discussion about what vehicles were in *The Traffic Jam* before handing out their open booklets and dictating the sentence to them. She has used a highlighter and marked one line for each word *I see a* and has written three sound boxes for the word *bus.*
Mrs. Jones: Yes, we are going to write four words. Touch the page where you will write the first word. What word are we going to write first?	Mrs. Jones watches to make sure everyone is touching the upper left-hand corner of the page on the first line. She moves a child's finger if they are not in the correct spot.
Group: I **Mrs. Jones:** Great! Write the word *I* now. (She waits until everyone writes the word *I*.) Now let's read what we wrote so we know what to write next. Be sure to point to the words as you read. **Group:** I see . . .	Mrs. Jones writes the same sentence on the large white board for all to see if they need the support.

FIGURE 4.13   (*Continued*)

Mrs. Jones: *See* . . . that's the next word we need to write. Who remembers what that word looks like? (Children begin to answer all at once.)	
Mrs. Jones: E.J. write it up here on your practice page. (E.J. writes the letter *c.*) **Mrs. Jones:** E.J. you remembered the name of the letter *c* sounds the same as the word *see.* Here are the letters to make the word *see.* Say the word *see* and listen for the sounds you hear. **E.J.:** /sssss/ /eeeee/. **Mrs. Jones:** What sound did you hear first? **E.J.:** /sssss/, *s*! **Mrs. Jones:** Yes! Now make the word *see* right here. (E.J. builds the word *see* on his practice page.) **Mrs. Jones:** You did it! Now write the word *see* on your practice page while everyone else writes it on their practice page.	Mrs. Jones has E.J. write the word on his practice page so she can intervene if any confusions occur. She has magnetic letters for the word *see* on hand in case a child needs the support.

Mrs. Jones has each child write the word *see* three or four times on their practice page in order to take it to fluency. Then she has them write it in their story while she writes it on her board. The group rereads the story again and writes the word *a* fast.

Mrs. Jones: Let's read it again and figure out what our last word is. **Group:** I see a bus. **Mrs. Jones:** *Bus* is our last word. I am going to draw three sound boxes in my story because they will help me figure out some of the letters in the word *bus.* Now, watch me touch one box for every sound in the word *bus*: /b/ /u/ /s/.	Mrs. Jones is careful to touch one sound box, in order from left to right, for each sound in the word *bus.*

FIGURE 4.13 (*Continued*)

<table>
<tr>
<td rowspan="2"></td>
<td>

Mrs. Jones: I have already drawn your sound boxes for you. Together, touch your sound boxes and make the sounds you hear in *bus*.
Group: /b/ /u/ /s/.
Mrs. Jones: That was great! Let's do it again. Touch the boxes and say *bus*.
Group: /b/ /u/ /s/.
Mrs. Jones: This time, we are going to stop with the sound in the first box. Put your finger in the first box, say the word *bus*, what sound do you hear?
Group: /b/!
Mrs. Jones: Yes! I hear /b/ too. /b/ /b/ /b/ like bear on our ABC chart. So, what letter would we write?
Group: *b*!

</td>
<td>

Mrs. Jones keeps a careful eye on those students she thinks might need extra support matching the sounds to one box.

</td>
</tr>
<tr>
<td>

Mrs. Jones: I'm going to write the letter *b* in the first box in my story. You write the letter *b* in the first box in your story.
(Mrs. Jones waits until everyone has put a *b* in their first box.)

</td>
<td>

Mrs. Jones chooses to model writing one letter at a time in her sound boxes right along with the children.

</td>
</tr>
</table>

Mrs. Jones leads the children in using the sound boxes to hear the next two sounds in *bus*. For each letter, they begin at the first box, touch one box for each sound, and write the next letter they hear. They refer to the ABC chart if someone needs help linking a letter to the sound they hear. Once they have written the entire word, Mrs. Jones has the children slide their finger under the word *bus* and look at the sounds as they say it. This helps to ensure they notice the word looks right and sounds right. She has them finish by reading the story again and drawing a quick picture.

Component: Letter Learning
Focus: Learn new letter names and sounds; build automaticity with partially known and known letters and sounds

Mrs. Jones has set up magnetic letter trays to practice some letter sorting. Each child's tray has the upper case and lowercase letters from their name along with letters they have learned together as a group. She begins the letter-learning portion by having the children start with something they know, their names. Mrs. Jones watches to see how

FIGURE 4.13   (*Continued*)

quickly the children can grab the letters in their name from a sea of letters and build it. If a child is struggling, she may narrow the search field by:

- saying the color of the letter they are looking for.
- choosing two letters and saying, "Is it this letter or this letter?"
- circling a small number of letters that includes the letter they are looking for.

Once the children have built their name, she has them check it quickly with their finger and their eyes. Then she moves them into a letter-sorting activity.

<u>Student and Teacher Interactions</u>	<u>Teacher Moves and Rationale</u>
Mrs. Jones: Now, some of these letters have *circles* on them and some of them don't. Can you pick up a letter that has a *circle*? **Karie**: *a* has a circle! **Johnny:** *o*! **E.J.:** *o*! **Aubrey:** *b* has a circle! **Mrs. Jones:** Great! Now find a letter that doesn't have a circle. **Johnny:** *y*! **Aubrey:** *A*! **Karie:** *K*! **E.J.:** *E*!	Mrs. Jones chooses to sort magnetic letters because the task gives the children opportunities to look closely at and compare different attributes of letters.
Mrs. Jones: All of you picked letters that did not have a circle. Now, sort all your letters on your tray into letters that have a circle and letters that don't have a circle. (Children work at sorting and naming their letters.)	Mrs. Jones watches the children carefully and assists with any letter confusions. She stops children occasionally to ask them to quickly name the letters that have a circle or the letters that do not have a circle. This provides an opportunity for children to build automaticity with letter naming in an engaging, playful way.
Mrs. Jones: Thank you for working so hard today! You may put your letters away.	

FIGURE 4.13

Learning How to Monitor and Solve

Mrs. Jones has been progress monitoring letter identification every two weeks for Aubrey, Karie, E.J., and Johnny. Now, all four students can consistently name at least forty-five letters. That means the skills focus during their small group time can now shift from learning letter names to solidifying letter sounds, building a bank of high frequency words, and working with more difficult words in word study. Authentically calling upon these skills will become imperative as children grow in their reading and writing.

Each week, Mrs. Jones takes running records *(McGee et al. 2015)* that allow her to see exactly what each child can do while reading and what they need to learn next. As she makes decisions about moving children up from levels A and B to level C, she looks for consistent use of directionality and one-to-one voice-to-print matching. At the same time, she's also looking for evidence that students are noticing high frequency words in texts and possibly beginning to monitor any voice-to-print mismatches with them. From looking at Aubrey's, Karie's, E.J.'s, and Johnny's running records of the book titled *Big House, Little Mouse*, she's gathered the information about each reader shown in Figure 5.1.

From observing her children during small group and analyzing her running records, Mrs. Jones knows there is a little shifting that needs to take place within her small groups. Both E.J. and Aubrey are ready to take on the new challenges found in Level C books. So, she will move them to another group with Deedra and TaShawn who are in similar places in their reading journeys. Karie and Johnny need a bit more time working in harder Level B books or possibly even some easy Level C books.

→

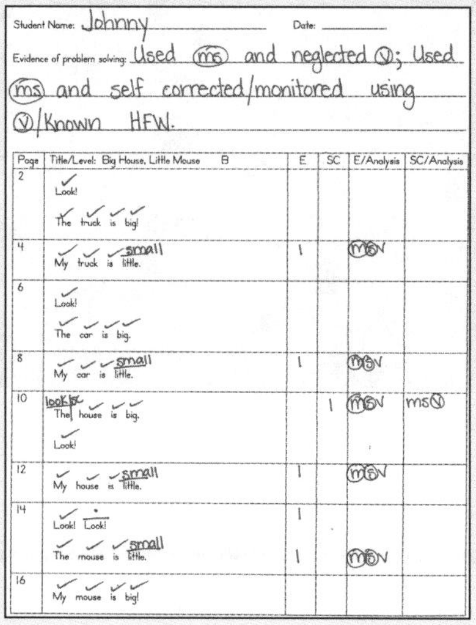

➤ Johnny
  ✔ demonstrated correct left-to-right directionality with a return sweep back to the left on two lines of text.
  ✔ controlled one-to-one voice-to-print matching.
  ✔ used meaning and structure but neglected print information when reading *small* for *little* each time it appeared in the story.
  ✔ monitored a high frequency word and self-corrected the error when he read *look* for *the*.
  ✔ omitted one word.
  ✔ made five errors.

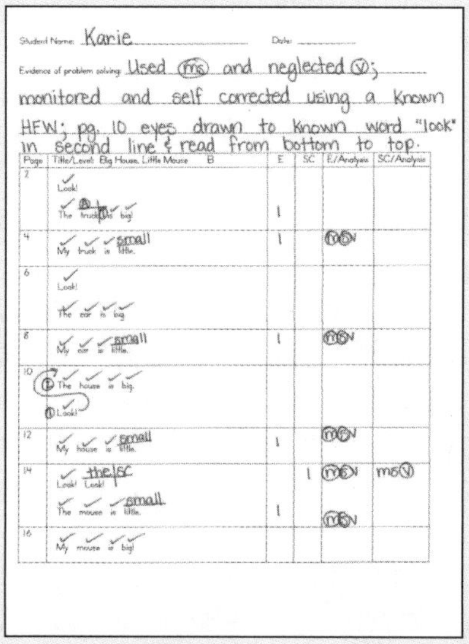

➤ Karie
  ✔ demonstrated correct left-to-right directionality with a return sweep back to the left on two lines of text except on one page. Her eyes were drawn to the word *look* on the second line, she continued the book's pattern and correctly read both lines of text from the left to right but incorrectly from bottom to top.
  ✔ controlled one-to-one voice-to-print matching.
  ✔ appealed for help one time (truck) and got told the word by her teacher.
  ✔ used meaning and structure but neglected print information when reading *small* for *little* each time.
  ✔ monitored a high frequency word and self-corrected the error when she read *the* for *look*.
  ✔ made five errors.

FIGURE 5.1

Students' Running Records and Teacher Comments

➤ E.J.
  ✔ demonstrated correct left-to-right directionality with a return sweep back to the left on two lines of text.
  ✔ controlled one-to-one voice-to-print matching.
  ✔ was able to monitor using the initial letter sound when he said /s/ and correctly read the word *little*.
  ✔ made no errors.
➤ Aubrey
  ✔ demonstrated correct left-to-right directionality with a return sweep back to the left on two lines of text.
  ✔ controlled one-to-one voice-to-print matching.
  ✔ used meaning and structure but neglected print information when she read *van* for *truck* two times.
  ✔ used meaning and structure when she read *small* for *little* and self-corrected the error using print information. She most likely noticed *little* couldn't be *small* from the first letter.
  ✔ made no errors.

FIGURE 5.1 (*Continued*)

Karie needs to solidify the top-to-bottom directionality of two lines of print. Both children need more practice looking closer at print. And although monitoring and self-correcting will not be priorities for them just yet, Mrs. Jones hopes Karie and Johnny will at least begin to notice when a word doesn't look right and maybe even pause a moment to look closer. Mrs. Jones will search her book baskets—both B and C—to find just the right books that will help scaffold Karie's and Johnny's learning.

CHAPTER 5

Teachers who are very successful at the small group table have a comprehensive understanding of reading theory, the *why* behind what they are teaching. They also know their children well, know their book collection well, and rely on useful formative assessments to guide them in making the right decisions at the right time for their early readers. Let's review what our readers should already control as they leave Levels A and B and then take a look at the new supports you can put in place that will keep young readers afloat in the unpatterned texts of Level C (see Figure 5.2).

There's no way to sugar coat it—the move out of patterned texts is a big one. The transition from Level B to Level C probably gives young children (and their teachers) the biggest challenges in the journey through early reading levels. Why is this so tricky? Let's go back to our swimming analogy. At some point the swim instructor has to let some air out of the floaties so swimmers can start floating on their own. Levels A and B texts held the reader up with patterned sentences, just as floaties do. Now, however, it's time for readers to learn the art of holding themselves up in the water. Reducing reliance on language patterns

What does the child know and control?	What is the child ready to learn?
■ Enjoys listening to picture books being read aloud	■ More high frequency words
■ Makes connections and loves to talk when listening to a book	■ Return sweep back to the left on two or more lines of text
■ Knows readers turn the pages of a book	■ How to monitor using known high frequency words
■ With support, can tell an oral story that has a beginning, middle, and end	■ How to use the initial letter and sound to monitor attempts at unknown words
■ Can draw a simple story and is beginning to use a variety of colors	■ How to use initial letter and sound to solve unknown words that are not simple CVC (consonant-vowel-consonant) words
■ Usually can write their first name	
■ Knows print contains the message	
■ Can locate their name in print	■ How to hear sounds in sequence when attempting to write simple, one-syllable words
■ Practices left-to-right directionality across one line of text	
■ Consistently uses one-to-one voice-to-print matching	■ How to solve CVC words within meaningful text
■ Knows more than 45 letter names and consonant sounds	

FIGURE 5.2

Learners Who Are Ready for Level C Texts

encourages them to start holding themselves afloat with more print information and its relation to sounds in words. In a nutshell, the work in this next band of text levels will be about refining how closely children look at print and helping them find footholds to guide their reading attempts.

We know that when we deflate floaties, young swimmers need enough skill to compensate for the decreased support. We teach swimmers to kick their legs. We teach them how to move their arms. We tell them to relax! (Ever seen a panicked swimmer in the water?!) The same holds true for what we must do for readers of unpatterned text. We have to show them what footholds (known words or letters) to use. We have to show them how to handle the unfamiliar parts.

You may have noticed that in the patterned text of Levels A and B, readers were able to navigate the print simply by using a general knowledge of how print works. If they could move consistently left to right and could match a spoken word to a printed word (even if they couldn't read those words in isolation), they could read most Level A and B books. Moving forward, they'll use an increasing amount of print information to read the unpatterned books found in Level C and above. Readers will need to be on the lookout for words they know, since those words won't appear in the same place on every page. Readers will encounter words they've never seen and will need to use bits of knowledge about letters, sounds, and meaning to solve them. The goal is to help our readers notice and use more details in print. They are usually ready for this if their directional skills and one-to-one matching are secure and require less of their conscious attention.

Sometimes, however, the transition from fully inflated floaties to partially inflated floaties is a rough one. It's not unusual for some children to find it difficult to process the print of unpatterned books. Sometimes they don't have enough footholds, such as high frequency words and known letter sounds, to monitor their reading. Sometimes they have a difficult time locating what they know embedded in larger amounts of print. So just as a panicked swimmer might flounder wildly, a panicked reader might resort to making up the story, even abandoning their known skill of one-to-one matching. As the lifeguard here, your job is to remain calm and not panic yourself. Often teachers will at this point take their readers back to patterned text. Try to avoid this. Putting the swimmer back in the baby pool is usually not the answer. You don't want to perpetuate the idea that reading relies on memorizing a pattern, so you'll have to help bridge this transition.

A guiding principle that might help you here is if one level becomes very easy, with accurate reading rates of close to 100 percent, students need to move to the next level, even if that level is too hard at first. Guided reading instruction should meet children at the point where the text has enough challenge for them to need instruction and scaffolding. Staying in too low a level will not provide the challenge. We need to get them to their zone of proximal development and this may mean providing extra supports when moving to a tougher level. Don't think of it as cheating. Think of it as a gradual release of responsibility, which is good teaching.

If (actually, *when*) you have children who are unsuccessful in their attempts at this next band of levels, you can teach some transitional lessons. These lessons will scaffold them as they learn to juggle looking for and using what they know about print with maintaining attention to meaning and language structures.

FROM THE SHALLOW END TO THE DEEP END: A SUGGESTED TRANSITION LESSON FORMAT

When your readers are having difficulties getting over the hump into Level C texts, consider using the following lesson formats that allow them to move to Level C, but with enough supports in place for them to be able to focus on the story with confidence and enjoyment. The supports included in this set of lessons are slowly decreased across three days so that your readers can take on increasing responsibility for using the print on their own. (Remember, we're slowly deflating their floaties.) You'll want to note that in this suggested set of transition lessons, the same new book is read repeatedly with support before we ask students to try it on their own (see Figure 5.3).

As you look over Figure 5.3, you'll notice some familiar components, such as writing, word learning, and letter learning, and these will continue throughout the lessons you'll teach to transition readers from Level B to Level C texts. What's different in this lesson progression is the scaffolded support readers will get for their new book.

Gradual Release Model with a New Book

In this model, children will have had experience with the new book four times before you ask them to read it on their own. For two days, they will experience the book twice within the same lesson. You can be as flexible as you wish, depending on your students' responses. Perhaps a group will need this much support for their first few Level C books, but then will be ready for you to reduce the number of exposures before reading on their own. Other groups may need more or less support. As always, stay aware of and responsive to your students' needs. Any scaffolds put in place should be removed as quickly as possible so readers can become as independent as possible. Fisher and Frey's (2014) gradual release model allows the reader to observe an expert navigate the challenges of the book and perhaps point out the helpful footholds along the way. In this nonthreatening setting, you can give your readers a heads up about the known words and the new words with known letter sounds they can use to navigate the book. Let's take a closer look at how to transition from you reading the new book to your children reading the book across the three-day lesson

Day 1	Day 2	Optional Day 3
New Book: Read TO	New Book: Read WITH	New Book: Read On your Own
New Book: Read WITH	New Book: Partner Read	Writing: Includes Word Learning and Letter Learning
Word Learning	Word Learning	
Letter Learning	Letter Learning	

FIGURE 5.3

Text Level C Transition Lesson Cycle

cycle included in Figure 5.3. Notice the gradual release of teacher support as you move through each stage.

New Book: Read TO

Start with a short introduction of the book as you traditionally would with your classroom read-alouds. Give an overarching statement about the book to help students connect to and understand the gist, for example: *"This is a book about a family trying to wake up a sleepy dad. We'll see if they are able to wake him up!"* Hold a copy of the book up for the group to see and read it to them. Your goal here is to acclimate your students to the meaning, language, and structure of the book.

New Book: Read WITH

Now, hand each student a copy of the book and read the text with them very slowly, keeping an eye on their fingers and their eyes. Look for them to be accurately following along and reading any parts they can. Let your voice hesitate or trail off on any parts you think they can read on their own. This gives them a bit of confidence that they can do some of the reading on their own. Model strategies for solving unknown words by starting the first sound of the word and elongating it, but give them room to say the word before you do. You are showing them what to do when they encounter tricky parts on their own.

New Book: PARTNER Read

Partner reading is a valuable technique to teach your students because you can use it at the guided reading table and for independent reading in the classroom, and it allows the students to take a step away from teacher support before trying a book on their own. Show students what this looks and sounds like by modeling it yourself with one of the students.

- *When we partner read, we sit shoulder to shoulder.*
- *When we partner read, we use a quiet whispery voice.*
- *When we partner read, we point to each word.*
- *When we partner read, we stay together with our friend as we read. We never leave a friend behind.*
- *When we partner read and we are both stuck on a tricky part, we ask for help from the teacher.*

New Book: Read on your OWN

Next, invite students to read their copy of the new book on their own with a soft voice. *Stagger start* the students on their reading so that they are not on the same pages at the beginning. You can achieve a staggered start in a few ways. You can hand out the books one by one, letting each child read a page before handing the next child a book. You can hand out a book to every other child, have them start to read, then hand out the rest. At this point, you don't want the group to be choral reading anymore because they now need to be thinking on their own. Lean in and listen to your readers for a short time, in random order, to prompt and help them as needed.

During these transitional lessons, be on constant lookout for when your readers are ready to move on to the regular lesson format. If they're gaining confidence and contributing more and more, it's time to pull back. Perhaps you'll choose not to read the book to the group, instead giving them a thorough introduction and then choral reading the book with the children. Perhaps you will try to eliminate the partner reading. The important thing is to take away these scaffolds as quickly as you can and move on to the regular Level C lesson format.

MY CHILDREN HAVE DIRECTIONALITY AND ONE-TO-ONE MATCHING UNDER CONTROL. NOW WHAT?

Once the foundational skills of direction and one-to-one word matching are under control, the real fun begins, in our opinion. We love teaching children with Level C text because almost every book gives them opportunities to use what they know strategically. You'll see readers noticing errors, sometimes fixing them, and using both print and picture to figure out unknown words.

Typically, readers stay in Level C books for a bit longer than other levels because of the amount of practice needed in these new areas, so we like to build up a rather extensive collection of books at Level C and the easiest Level D books. To further support this, we'll focus a great deal on helping children develop "strategic actions" (Clay 2001) around five areas for problem solving as students learn to check on themselves for accuracy and understanding and figure out words they don't recognize in print. We'll talk about the checking behaviors, or *monitoring*, first.

Using What You Know in Print to Monitor

Emergent readers must learn to monitor their reading—to observe themselves, check on themselves, and keep their reading under systematic review. Monitoring doesn't necessarily mean fixing. Readers have to know something is wrong before they can fix it, so we will applaud our readers for noticing errors, even if they can't fix them yet. Of course, if they happen to notice and fix a mistake independently, or *self-correct*, we'll be even more excited for our problem-solving reader. First monitoring experiences usually are about checking on one-to-one word matching, but in Level C, the monitoring gets more complex. We want to see readers monitoring the high frequency words they know and the first letters of words they attempt.

Using What You Know in Print to Solve Unknown Words

Solving unknown words in print is a complex undertaking. Some might think *solving* is synonymous with *decoding*, but we would disagree. Solving, of course, does involve decoding, but not decoding alone. The solving that ultimately matters to readers is the solving done while maintaining the meaning of the text. Readers should use both sources of information right from the start. We will discuss what solving should look like in Level C books and how we can help our children become readers who try something when faced with an unknown word in print.

Hearing Sounds in Language and Matching Sounds to Letters

Readers of Level C texts and above must learn to hear sounds in words (*phonemic awareness*) and begin matching those sounds to letters (*phonics*). Keep in mind that the relationship between print and speech goes two ways. Literacy requires us to be able to translate sounds we hear in words and match them to printed letters, as we do when writing. Conversely, it also requires us to see printed letters and match them to sounds in order to read. As mentioned before, in our experience, we've often found it's easier for many children to learn how to use their letter sound knowledge in writing than in reading. We'll discuss this again in more detail in the writing section of this chapter, but perhaps children find the slower nature of writing easier and more explicit. In general, children reading Level C books should be able to hear and write the sounds for simple three-letter and four-letter words. Vowels may be confused, but children should be including some vowels in their writing. The skills practiced first in writing can then be called on for reading.

Learning Words

Learning high frequency words plays several important roles in early literacy. We talked earlier about the importance of *monitoring* in reading. It's really hard to monitor if you don't have some known items in the print, and the more you know, the more you can monitor. Having some parts of the text they can read automatically without effort helps readers reserve some energy for the harder parts that need more work. This also allows some of the reading to go quickly and sound like natural speech. We aren't sticklers for numbers but feel recognizing approximately thirty useful high frequency words by the time they move into Level D or Level E text is a reasonable goal.

Practicing Letters and Sounds

Early readers should continue to firm up their knowledge of letter names, sounds, and formations. Many of your students at this point may know most or all letter names and many sounds. Continue to provide practice opportunities so that letters and sounds become known with very little conscious attention and increasing automaticity. When you think letters and sounds are known, practice a little bit more!

KEY CHARACTERISTICS OF LEVEL C TEXTS

Just as we saw variances in the characteristics of Levels A and B, books in the next level band are not created equal. The books in your Level C basket will vary in complexity, length, and difficulty. You'll find some Level C books are on par with your harder Level Bs, so remember to look across your baskets. There are key text features you will find especially helpful when teaching children how to handle unpatterned texts. Choose books that provide the opportunities to practice new skills, while continuing to reinforce skills that are now easy for the reader, keeping in mind the following features that help children learn to look more closely at print and use what they know to monitor their reading.

- Since children need to be able to navigate increasingly larger quantities of print, some pages should have more than two lines of print.
- Most pages should deviate from the patterned language structures found in earlier levels. Children are learning to monitor print information and too much pattern gives them the wrong idea about reading. We don't want them thinking memorizing a language pattern is the goal.

CHAPTER 5

- Some pages should feel easier, with, perhaps, fewer words or a bit of patterned language. These pages provide a sigh of relief for children who have worked very hard on the longer pages.
- Building a large core of *sight words* is important, so known high frequency words should appear throughout the book and a few new ones should be introduced.
- There should be several opportunities to solve simple new words, using at least the first letter (or more) and the context of the story.
- Books should contain a simple story structure with characters, plot, and sometimes dialogue.

Again, when choosing books for your small group, we caution you to avoid books that:

- can be easily memorized because of too much patterned language.
- are so highly decodable that a single phonics principle dictates word choice.

When we discussed text characteristics of great Level A and B books, we mentioned lightbulb moments that indicate readers are successfully managing the challenges of those particular books. In Levels A and B, we looked for ease with directional movement and automatic one-to-one word matching. Our lightbulb moments in Level C include strategic behaviors that show monitoring and solving with items students know, while maintaining meaning. As summarized above, texts that support these goals will have limited pattern, more high frequency words, and a few words to solve using both print information (letters and sounds) and meaning.

TEACHING WITH LEVEL C TEXTS

As readers take on Level C texts, they begin to see themselves as real readers because they know they are using the print to figure out what to say. The stories become meatier, so our conversations about the books become meatier as well. When we work with readers in these books, we divide our focus into two main categories: learning *items* and learning *how to use* those items.

Items
- high frequency words
- automaticity with letter names and sounds

Using the items
- monitoring and self-correcting known high frequency words
- monitoring, self-correcting, and solving with the first letter of unknown words
- using sound analysis to encode and decode two-letter and three-letter words with short vowels (V-C, C-V-C)
- doing all these things while monitoring and solving using meaning and language structure

Once again, we provide a two-day lesson cycle with an optional third day (Figure 5.4). However, you understand your children best so feel free to adapt to meet your children's needs. Since we know that different teachers meet with their guided reading groups different numbers of times per week, we've provided an optional lesson format for Day 3 that can be repeated for Day 4 and Day 5 if you see a group every day. The flexible nature of this optional lesson gives you the gift of time—time to squeeze in whatever teaching you feel is the most important for that group.

CHAPTER 5

Day 1	Day 2	Optional Day 3
Familiar Reading	Reread Book from Day 1	Familiar Reading
New Book: ■ Teacher introduces the book. ■ Students whisper read or partner read. High Frequency Words: ■ Fluency Practice ■ Learn a New Word	High Frequency Words: ■ Fluency Practice ■ Review New Word from Day 1	High Frequency Words: ■ Review Words ■ Assess words as needed
Letter and Sound Practice OR Word Study (phonemic awareness and phonetic development)	Writing	Letter and Sound Practice OR Word Study (phonemic awareness and phonetic development)

FIGURE 5.4
Text Level C Lesson Cycle

Maybe you notice they are inconsistent with some high frequency words and they need some extra practice. Maybe you notice that sound boxes aren't going well and you want some concentrated time to practice that procedure. Maybe you would like to have them write a bit more about the book. These optional lessons let you decide what needs extra work without taking time to introduce and read another new book. Rereading familiar books is always an incredibly valuable use of instructional time, so it makes sense if you decide you want to give that component plenty of time. However, if you'd like to introduce more than one new book per week, you can cycle back to a Day 1 lesson, rather than move on to a Day 3 lesson. You know best what your students need, so be flexible and follow their lead. We'll walk through each lesson component below.

Introducing the New Book

Because of the new challenges at Level C, your first book introductions will likely need to offer quite a bit of information. Then once your group adjusts to the complexity, you'll be able to pull back a bit on this level of support. At first, you'll need to guide them in noticing that not every page of these books will have the same language pattern. You'll need to remind

CHAPTER 5

them of their footholds in print (known words and letters) which will help them read exactly what the author wrote. You'll be the judge of how much support to give, but we'll give you some ideas of areas that may need more support at first.

Let's look at *A Bike for Russ*, a Level C book, and think about how this book might be introduced to readers who are new to the challenges of Level C texts.

Big Idea

Level C books have some pretty great storylines and are often very relatable to children's own experiences. As always, give your readers a heads-up about what the book is generally about and how it works. Sometimes it's also a good idea to solicit predictions about the story from the cover. (Often, it's not a good idea, and we'll talk about that shortly as well.) Take a look at the cover of *A Bike for Russ.* The cover clearly shows his bike is too small for him (Figure 5.5). You might say, "Here is your new book, *A Bike for Russ.* This story is about a boy named Russ and he has a problem with his bike. This problem happens to a lot of children. Do you see what his problem is?"

This opening statement captures the main idea of the story, allows children to think about what the picture might indicate, and allows some of them to make a personal connection. This is exactly what you want. Asking them to draw conclusions from this picture is a pretty safe bet because the picture is clear about the nature of the boy's problem. A word of caution, however, is necessary about asking children to make predictions about the story from the cover at this level. If the picture is ambiguous, the predictions can get way off the mark. This is a common problem when children first encounter Level C books. Their cognitive challenge

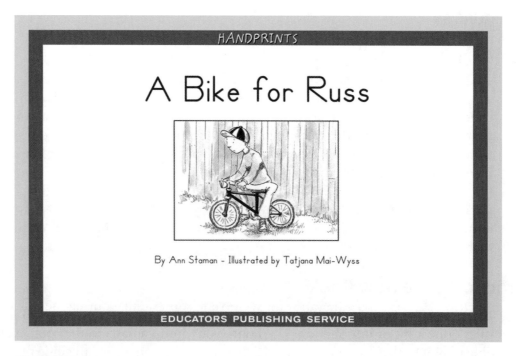

FIGURE 5.5
A Bike for Russ, *Cover*

is going to be monitoring print information with unpatterned language—so it's very helpful if the meaning of the story is clear. If you invite too much talk about unrelated connections or way-off predictions, you could be adding a challenge by confusing the meaning. Keep the discussion pretty tight at this point. Have a short (very short!) discussion about how he has outgrown his bike and needs a bigger bike. Some children may share that this has happened to them.

Meaning and Language Structure

Now begin to guide your students through the book, revealing the major plot episodes as you go. For new readers of Level C, you'll want to take care to use some of the language of the book and sometimes have the children rehearse the language as well. If your readers rehearse some of the book language, such as dialogue, it will be easier for them to handle when they have to reconstruct it from print on their own. Later, as they become more proficient, you won't need to provide as many of these opportunities.

Here's an example of what you might say to new readers of Level C to support language structure, as you introduce *A Bike for Russ* on pages 14 to 15. See Figure 5.6.

"Let's turn the page and see what the twins are showing Russ. Do you think they found a good bike for Russ? I think so too! That looks like it might work. So, the twins said, 'Here is a bike.' Let's read that page together now. You know the first word, so put your finger under it and get ready to read. The . . . twins . . . said . . . Here . . . is . . . a . . . bike. Great. Now let's turn to see what Russ thinks of this bike."

FIGURE 5.6
A Bike for Russ, *Pages 14 to 15*

Print Information

Select a place or two in the print for your readers to examine during the introduction. You have some choices (as always) about where you want to direct their attention but try to stay focused on the learning goals at this level and think about the level of support your readers need. You may decide to look at a couple of words your readers could solve with a bit of a scaffold, but maybe not on their own. You may also choose to point out a high frequency word or two as a reminder for your readers to monitor. Below are a few places where you might do this while introducing *A Bike for Russ.*

- *High frequency word: Here*
  "The twins are showing Russ a bike that might work for him. Take a look at what they say. Do you see the word *Here*? Put your finger under it and read it. That word will help you read this page."
- *First letter to solve a new word: twins*
  "Russ's brothers are twins. This book calls them 'the twins.' What letter will you see at the beginning of the word *twins*? Say it. Yes, now find it and read the word *twins*."
- *Simple, regularly spelled word: Russ*
  "If you forget this character's name, you can use the letter sounds to figure it out. Let's look at his name. If his name were in sound boxes, how would you say it? Run your finger under it and look at those sounds while you read his name with me. R-r-r-u-u-u-s-s-s."

Concluding Statement

As you have been doing all along, give a brief statement to remind students of the big idea of the book and then a quick reminder of what they need to do as readers.

"You're ready to read about Russ and his search for just the right bike. Remember to check for the words you know. And if you're not sure of a word, the first letter will help you decide."

Reading the New Book

Children can now begin whisper reading their books on their own, at their own pace. Before you settle in to listen individually to each child, make sure they are all reading at their own pace instead of choral reading with their neighbor. Keep a dry erase marker and some magnetic letters handy for any on-the-spot teaching you may need to do for an individual child. You can whisper a bit of praise or give a quiet thumbs up when things are going smoothly, and you'll probably need to do some prompting and teaching during this first reading. Here are some suggestions for how to scaffold at Level C.

Teaching and Prompting During Reading

If a skill is brand new or particularly confusing for a reader, you'll want to offer higher levels of support. You may need to demonstrate, share the task, or prompt very specifically. As the child's skill increases, you'll want to pull back. Choose prompts that give less information, allowing the child as much independence as possible. Here are some support suggestions for our learning focuses for Level C and the easier Level D texts.

Monitoring Known Words

In Level C texts, you'll want to show students that looking carefully at the print will reward them with familiar words, to be read easily and with certainty. Help them learn to slow down, check the print, and actively search for what they know.

- Have the child find what he knows on the page before reading it in context. It is not unusual for words known in isolation or on flashcards to go unnoticed when surrounded by more print and within a meaningful message. You don't want to make this a habit, so reserve it just for children who are new to finding what they know in print. And, like all scaffolds, remove it as soon as possible.
- If known high frequency words are misread, pull them out from the page and make them larger and clearer. You can either write the word on a whiteboard or make it with magnetic letters. Have the child read the word in isolation, then return to read the page with the word embedded in text.
- If a known high frequency word is misread, have the child reread the page, as you point. Instead of moving on when they miscue on the high frequency word, direct their attention back to the word by tapping if you need to.
- If a known high frequency word is misread, prompt the child to take action. Try starting with the least specific prompt, giving more direction as needed, ranging from "Try that again." to "A word you know is tricking you on this page. Try this page again."

Monitoring First Letters

Children reading Level C books will have been using their letter sound knowledge quite a bit in writing and now it's time for them to put this knowledge to work in reading. *Monitoring* using first letter sounds tends to be easier than *solving* using first letter sounds, so we will call on this first. Both are developing simultaneously but solving is much more complex than deciding if an attempt is correct by checking the first sound. Help your readers practice attending to the first letter as their mouth draws out the first sound, in order to check.

- Demonstrate how to check a meaningful attempt at an unknown word. First, praise them for making an attempt that makes sense. Then have them say their attempt and listen to the first sound. Ask what letter that word would start with or ask them what letter they would use first to write that word. Then ask them to check in print for the first letter of the unknown word. Could they be right? For example, if a child reads 'ladybug' for 'bug,' try saying this: *"You said 'ladybug.' That makes sense! Now, say it again and think. What letter would you see at the beginning of 'ladybug?' Check it. Oh, this word starts with a 'b' so it can't be ladybug. Good checking!"*
- Have the child reread the page with the misread word, as you point to the words. Instead of moving on when they make the error, tap the first letter, or cover all but the first letter of the word, or show them a magnetic letter of the first sound. "Why can't it be 'ladybug'?"
- Rather than telling them the word directly, give them a choice. This requires them to do some thinking. For instance, you might say, *"Is it 'bug' or 'ladybug'? How do you know?"*
- You might also help them access their knowledge from writing, asking, *"What letter would you write first for 'ladybug?' Can this be 'ladybug'?"*

Solving Unknown Words with First Letters (or More) and Meaning

Children reading Level C text are beginning to venture into an area that requires a rather complex skill—integrating more than one source of information. Think aloud to show your students how you simultaneously think about meaning as you start articulating the sounds of the

CHAPTER 5

unknown word. Connect their skills of analyzing sounds when writing new words to blending sounds in reading. This skill becomes firmer in Level D, but don't wait to get to Level D before you start modeling and encouraging your readers to try it in the easier texts of Level C.

- You can model this for the whole group or just teach this individually to students in your group who seem ready. Find a simply spelled word to solve (for example, CVC), embedded in meaningful text.

  "If I wasn't sure what this word was, here's what I would do. I would read this sentence again and then quickly make the first sound of the tricky word. I bet we can think what makes sense that starts that way. Watch me do it."

- When first letters are easy and sound boxes are going well in writing, encourage readers to start using these skills beyond the first letter to solve unknown words in their books.

  "Listen to me say these sounds together. You run your finger under it and I'll make the sounds. Let's read this sentence again and see if it makes sense."

  "If this word were in sound boxes, how would you say it?"

- When they are more independent:

  "What makes sense that starts that way?"

  "What sounds do you see?"

  "Can you say more of it? Would that make sense?"

  "Try it."

Like all good teaching, your demonstrations and prompts will change as students become more experienced with these skills. In Figure 5.7 we summarize some of the changes in prompts you can use.

Teaching Points After the Reading

After reading the book, enjoy a short conversation about the book, with no particular agenda, just as friends might talk about a book. You might talk about surprises, funny parts, or connections. This could possibly be the most important teaching point you make—reading is pleasurable and it connects us through a joint experience.

Next, decide what clear point you want your readers to remember. Usually, this will relate to one of your big learning goals. So, at this level, think about opportunities to teach about monitoring and solving using known items. Your teaching point might just be verbal, or you might write on a chart or whiteboard, but your readers should refer to their books to put the teaching point in context. You can highlight good work done by one or all readers in the group, or you can just demonstrate using a page from the book that is a clear example of the learning goal. Remember less is more. Too much teaching will muddy, rather than clarify, your readers' thinking.

For instance, after reading the book *A Bike for Russ*, you might say, *"I noticed some of our sight words in this book. Did you? Show us a page where a word you know helped you"* (monitoring for high frequency words).

Or, *"I noticed some tricky words in this book that I don't think you've seen before. But you still could check them! Let's look at page 14. What helped you know that this word is* twins *and not* boys*? Yes,* boys *would start with* b *and this starts with the /t/ sound. Put your finger under the /t/ and let's read* twins *and look at the sounds. That's one way we check"* (monitoring for first letter of unknown words).

	Monitoring Known Words	Monitoring with First Letters	Solving Unknown Words with First Letters (or More) and Meaning
New behavior	<ul><li>Before reading: "Find the words you know on this page. Read them. Now read this page and when you point to those words, you'll know what to say."</li><li>When students misread a known word, make the word with magnetic letters or write it clearly with a dry-erase marker. "Do you know this word? Good, now find it on this page. Good. Now read the page again."</li><li>When children misread a known word: Have them reread the page, directing their attention back to the word in some way.</li><li>"Something didn't look right. There is a word you know on this page—check again for what you know. Do you see it? Good. Now try the page again."</li></ul>	<ul><li>"You said 'ladybug.' That makes sense! Now, say it again and think. What letter would you see at the beginning of 'ladybug?' Check it."</li><li>Have the child reread the page, as you point to the words, highlighting the first letter in some way. "Why can't it be 'ladybug'?"</li><li>"Is it 'bug' or 'ladybug'? How do you know?"</li><li>"What would you write first for 'ladybug?' Can this be 'ladybug'?"</li></ul>	<ul><li>"Let's read this sentence again and then quickly make the first sound of the tricky word. I bet we can think what makes sense that starts that way." You can model this the first few times and then do it with the child.</li><li>Is it "bug" or "ladybug?" How can you tell?</li><li>When first letters are easy and sound boxes are going well in writing: "Listen to me say these sounds together. You run your finger under it and I'll make the sounds." "If this word were in sound boxes, how would you say it?" "Now let's read the sentence again and see if it makes sense.</li></ul>
Inconsistent behavior	<ul><li>"A word you know is tricking you on this page. Try this page again."</li><li>"Something doesn't look right. Try this page again."</li></ul>	<ul><li>"Something doesn't look right. Check the first sounds."</li></ul>	<ul><li>"What makes sense that starts that way?"</li></ul>
Almost secure behavior	<ul><li>"Try that again."</li><li>"Were you right?"</li></ul>	<ul><li>"Try that again."</li><li>"Were you right?"</li></ul>	<ul><li>"Can you say more of it?"</li><li>"Try it."</li></ul>

FIGURE 5.7

Summary Table of Teaching with Level C

Or, *"This book has some new words that you've never seen before. Let's talk about how you can figure them out. Look at the last page, where Russ is on a bike he likes. Put your finger under the first word. What might he be saying that makes sense? Look at the first sound and think what he might say. /Y-y-y/yes! Yes would make sense! Now let's read again and check it"* (solving using the first letter and meaning).

Rereading Familiar Books

We've mentioned before the value in rereading, so we make sure to provide time for rereading familiar books in every guided reading lesson that does not include a new book. Commonly, teachers think of familiar reading as the perfect opportunity to work on fluency. And we agree—but with a couple of caveats. First, when readers first begin reading the unpatterned text of Level C books, they are practicing a brand-new skill—carefully checking for what they know about each printed word. We can't expect this to be done at speed right away. So, if you notice slow, word-by-word reading at this point, it's not necessarily a bad thing. You want to see this slowing down to check. Once you notice that your readers are monitoring for known words and some first letters, you can then expect them to put words together like talking. Don't worry so much about speed as you do about making the reading sound like natural speech.

As a second caution, be careful about providing patterned texts from Level A for familiar reading material. If your children have just moved out of patterned text, providing it again can disrupt the new monitoring skills you are trying to help them build. With this in mind, do your best to offer Level B and Level C options that are not patterned.

Learning High Frequency Words

Remember, high frequency words build a child's confidence when they look at a page filled with print. At this point, it becomes an especially high priority since the learning focus at this level is monitoring and learning to monitor depends on having something *to* monitor. Here, to the suggestions already discussed on Chapter 4, Learning Words, pages 64–66, we'll add a few teaching strategies for working with previously taught words.

Once children start racking up known words, you may find they forget some and confuse others. Don't despair! This is not unusual. The psychological term for this is *retroactive interference* (Underwood and Postman 1960) and it means new learning can muddle previously learned material, if it has not been practiced over a long time. This is the reason we suggest continuing exposure and practice of words (and letters) even when you observe the child responding correctly. Expect some words to be forgotten, make note when they are, and then arrange for some more practice.

By the time children are reading texts in Level C and above, they are beginning to establish a link between the sounds in words and the letters that represent the sounds. We sometimes tell children certain words just have to be remembered because they aren't able to be sounded out. This is actually only partially true. There is usually at least part of the word that has a simple sound-to-symbol correspondence. Point this out as you teach the word. If you are teaching the word *look* point out that the first and last sounds are easy sounds to hear and record. At this point, the diphthong of *oo* is above their level of phonics skill. So, a general principle might be to point out the parts of words that match the children's phonics skill and ask for remembering of the trickier parts.

Consider trying the following ideas along with your own ideas. These are just options, to be used at your discretion, since you are the expert on your children and what would work best in your classroom.

Procedures for Learning a New Word

The procedures for learning a new word do not really change from level to level. This should be a familiar process and children should know what to expect and be familiar with the routine of how to learn a new high frequency word. See Chapter 4, Procedures for Learning a New Word, pages 64–66 to revisit this process.

Procedures for Practicing Known and Partially Known Words

- **Personal high frequency word (or word wall) sheets**
  In the same way the whole class uses a word wall, you could periodically print out a sheet with the words you plan to teach your class, either for the month or the quarter, like the one in Figure 5.8. Give each child their own copy and invite them to highlight words on their sheet when those words are taught and learned in their guided reading group. Have children occasionally practice the highlighted words and keep their sheets handy during writing and show children how to use them as a self-checking resource.

a	b	c	d	e	f	g
a and at		cat can	dad dog			go
h	**i**	**j**	**k**	**l**	**m**	**n**
	I is it			like look	mom me my	no
o	**p**	**q**	**r**	**s**	**t**	**u**
on	play			see	to	up
v	**w**	**x**	**y**	**z**		
	we		you	zoo		

FIGURE 5.8

Example of Student High Frequency Word Chart. Words get highlighted once a child demonstrates they can read it and write it easily without much effort.

CHAPTER 5

- **Magnetic boards prepared with magnetic letters**
  Small magnetic boards can be prepared ahead of time with a collection of magnetic letters and used to practice high frequency words. You can organize this several ways. Sometimes, we prepare enough boards for each group member to have a board, and each board has the letters for a different word. The children make and read their word a few times, then everyone passes their board to the neighbor to their right. Each child now practices the word on their new board a few times, until it's time to pass again. This way, everyone gets to practice several words, and the boards can often be used with several groups who might be learning the same words. Another way to organize is to prepare enough boards for each child in the group but have enough letters to make two or three words. Again, have the children make and read words, then pass their boards. This gives them practice with more words and requires them to search their brain for what words the letters might make.
- **Dry erase peel-off sticky sheets (see Figure 5.9)**
  Keep dry erase markers and small erasers within reach so children can quickly practice a word or give it a try if they aren't sure. Sometimes when children encounter a word they can't remember, writing it out for them will jog their memory, and this is a great place for this purpose too. Writing words to make them more automatic or to try out a spelling should be a seamless, automatic part of the guided reading lesson. Make sure your workspace allows for this.

You may feel a bit overwhelmed when you think about the volume of words readers need to be able to recognize and how slowly they seem to accumulate for some children in early levels. But, don't carry the weight of teaching all these words on your shoulders at the guided reading table. First of all, over time, the route to learning words will continue to get easier. As children learn *how* to learn words, they learn to examine a word, match some sounds to letters (and some letters to sounds), notice the irregular parts, and commit the

FIGURE 5.9
A guided reading table can have dry erase stickers at each student's seat.

word to memory. As this process is practiced, the learning gets faster. They also learn how to use analogies to learn new words. For example, if you know the word *the* it will be easier to learn *them* and *then* because you have part of the word stored in memory already. And there's more good news—most children will begin learning words they see frequently (hence the name *high frequency words*) in the books they read. The more reading they do, the more times they will be exposed to high frequency words and the more likely they are to learn more and more words. And, while you'll definitely be taking steps to support all of this, you don't want your guided reading time to be overtaken by just learning words.

Letters and Sound Practice OR Word Study

Since this portion of your lesson is short timewise, you need to plan efficiently. If your children need more time firming up letter naming and letter sounds, it makes sense to spend a few minutes working on those skills. If your children are gaining automaticity with letter naming and letter sounds, however, move on to spending more and more of this time doing some word study. As always, what your children need will dictate what you plan.

Letters and Sound Practice

If your children need to practice letter naming and letter sound automaticity, consider choosing *one* of the following activities:

- *ABC chart chant.* We continue to use the ABC chart as a reference (see Figure 5.10). You can have children point to and chant the chart saying the letter name, letter sound, and picture cue. For example: a, /a/, apple; b, /b/, bear; c, /c/, cat . . . z, /z/, zipper.
- *Magnetic letter arrays.* On individual magnetic letter trays, line up a set of magnetic letters and give one tray to each child. Have the children start on the left and push each letter up while naming it quickly. Then have each child start on the left again and pull each letter down while making the letter sound quickly.
- *My Pile/Your Pile (Clay 2005b)* Once children have progressed to having just a set of twenty-six lowercase letter cards they can play this game using letter names or letter sounds. One lesson you may have them name the letters fast and another lesson they may make the letter sounds fast. Or you may have them do both as they go through their piles, naming the letter first followed by that letter's sound.

Word Study

Beginning around Level C, we add a word study component to our guided reading lessons that goes beyond learning high frequency words. This component helps readers explore how words work (Bear et al. 2019) so they can solve new words in their reading. Of course, when using these skills in whole texts, readers will also use meaning as they solve, but the purpose of this lesson component is to sharpen their use of print information. Word work should help support your learning goals for the texts your children are reading, so in text Level C, we want children to begin to:

1. Blend the sounds of CVC words to solve in reading and writing.
2. Monitor mismatches using first letter and sound in words that are not simple CVC words.

CHAPTER 5

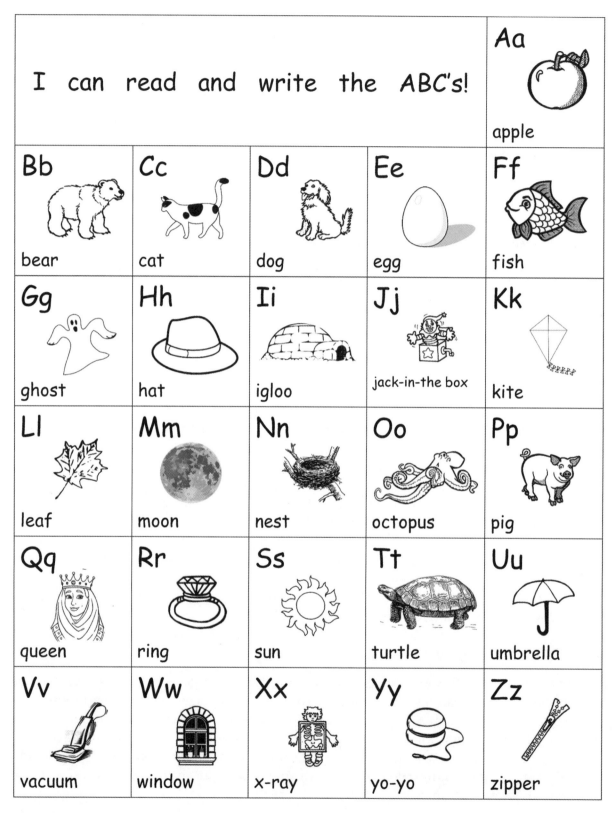

CHAPTER 5

FIGURE 5.10
ABC Chart

These simple goals actually require the ability to manipulate sounds and letters in a way that may be new to your readers, so make this very explicit. For example, children will focus on first letters in words both visually and orally. They will compare words that start with the same letter both visually and orally. And they will examine simple consonant–vowel–consonant (CVC) words by coordinating their eyes, ears, mouth, and finger letter by letter.

We recommend several activities using magnetic letters or sounds boxes (and sometimes both). Note that these aren't presented in a prescribed sequence. As the expert on your children, you will decide what activity or combination of elements will best meet the needs of your particular group on any particular day. We hope these activities will be a springboard in helping you see what your children need to learn. So, think about these ideas and then devise a plan that will best get your readers where they need to be.

Learning Goal Number One: Use the First Letter of Words to Monitor and Solve Words

Make Known Words with Magnetic Letters and Focus on the First Letter

In Level C, children will encounter some simple CVC words and you'll be teaching the skills needed to decode these words. These activities are meant to ensure children automatically attend to the first sound. Even when your children encounter words more complex than CVC, you don't want them to revert to guessing. You want them to automatically attend to the first letter(s).

Arrange for each child to have the magnetic letters needed to make a few known words. Choose the known words carefully. Your point is to examine the first letter sound, so you want the first letter sound to be a simple example, not a digraph, blend, or vowel. (Don't choose *the* or *in*.) If you have magnetic dry erase boards, you can have the letters ready on the boards. If not, you can have the letters in baggies or trays (we use dollar store stove burner covers!). See Figure 5.11.

Here are the steps we follow:

1. Ask children to make the first word. Watch that all children build words from left to right. Build the word on your board or table as well, as an example for any child who needs to see it (Figure 5.12).
2. Ask children to move the first letter of the word to the left, leaving a gap between the onset and the rime. Model by moving yours as well (Figure 5.13).
3. Ask children to put their pointing finger under the first letter, make the sound, and *in a fluid manner* run their finger under the rest of the word, reading the word in its entirety. The point is to see and hear the first sound in an exaggerated way, but not in a completely separated way. Try to go for *m-m-m-om* rather than *muh-om*. Practicing with words that start with sounds that can be elongated makes this process easier. Words that start with the letters *f, h, l, m, n, r, s, v, w, y*, and *z* are somewhat easier at first. With the other consonants, be careful not to add too much of a schwa sound to the end of the first sound to keep phonics work as close to sounding like words (and as far from sounding like a series of unrelated noises) as possible.
4. Ask children to then move the rime to the left next to the first letter, and read the whole word again, running their finger under it, left to right (Figure 5.14).

CHAPTER 5

FIGURE 5.11
Begin with magnetic letters in random order on a tray.

FIGURE 5.12
Children pull down the letters they need to build mom.

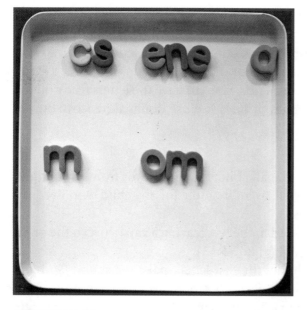

FIGURE 5.13
Children break mom *into onset and rime.*

FIGURE 5.14
Children put mom *back together and read it.*

In this activity, your job in this is to watch your readers' eyes. As you model, keep your eyes focused on theirs. Do they scan left to right? Do their eyes seem to really look at that first letter as they mouth it? Ask each child to read a word for you individually to see if their eyes and mouth are truly coordinated. Give quick feedback. "Oh, Xavier, make sure you look at the *m* when you're reading it. Let me see you read that again. I'm watching your eyes!"

Make Simple Words with Magnetic Letters and Focus on the First Letter

Now do this same activity but this time with words that are not necessarily fully known. Choose simple words from the stories they are reading that follow simple spelling patterns and are clear examples of how sounds and letters relate. With this less familiar word, follow the same process of breaking the first letter off to the left, pointing to and sounding the first letter and then reading the rest of the word before putting it all back together and reading the whole word. See Figure 5.15.

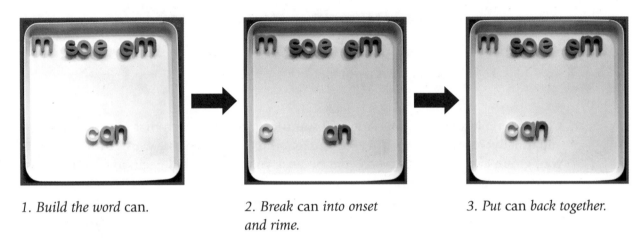

1. *Build the word* can.   2. *Break* can *into onset and rime.*   3. *Put* can *back together.*

FIGURE 5.15
Focusing on the First Letter With the Word can

Make Simple Words That Start With the Same Letter

Now do this same activity but make two or three words, all beginning with the same letter, in a column, each word under the other. Examples might be *mom, me, my* or *dad, dog, did* or *sun, so, said.*

1. Make the words, move the first sounds, and read each word as usual.
2. Ask the children what they notice.
3. Lead them to discover that when words look the same at the beginning, they often sound the same at the beginning. (Don't tell them letters *always* sound the same. Our language doesn't work that way.)
4. Ask them to notice what their mouth does at the beginning of each word. Is it the same? Would that help them read another new word that started the same way? Why, yes, it would!

Learning Goal Number Two: Blend the Sounds of Simple Three- and Four-Letter Words to Solve in Reading and Writing

Use Sound Boxes to Write or Make CVC Words

A way to make this skill more concrete and fun is to use magnetic letters with the sound box procedures you've used with your children in writing. This is just extra practice with hearing the sounds in words, matching them to letters, then reading them back. We usually write in sound boxes, but to change things up you can give children magnetic letters and let them push the magnetic letters in their corresponding sound boxes. See Figure 5.16.

CHAPTER 5

FIGURE 5.16
Sound Boxes for Map

1. Choose simply spelled words. You will want to start with words that have short vowels and usually words with two, three, or four letters. If you can choose words from the books your group has read, that's even better because your readers will begin to examine those words in print more closely.
2. Provide predrawn sound boxes for each child. As you do in the writing component, have the children say the word slowly, touching each box as they articulate each sound.
3. Fill in or push up the first sound.
4. Say the word slowly, touching each box again. Fill in or push up the second sound.
5. Continue saying the whole word slowly, touching each box from the beginning each time, filling in or pushing up sounds in order until the word is complete.
6. Have the children run their finger under the entire word, reading it slowly, and scanning it with their eyes. Your job is to watch for coordination of eyes, mouth, and finger.

Make CVC Words from Books with Magnetic Letters

Select a few words from the books you're using in guided reading that follow a CVC spelling pattern. As you've done before, arrange for your children to have the letters they need to make two or three of these words on a magnetic board or the table. You'll make these words one at a time, so the children can carefully examine each word without being visually distracted by any other words.

Tell the children the word you are going to make. Ask them to stretch the word with you. Some teachers call this "talking like a ghost." Some call it "turtle talk." Whatever you call it, your point is to help children say the word slowly enough to hear the component sounds. If they isolate each sound completely, it makes it more difficult in the actual act of reading whole text to hear the sounds as a meaningful word. So, if you can keep the sounding as close to the sound of a word as possible, you're doing your readers a favor. Once you have stretched the word, build it with your magnetic letters. At first, you may want to build the word letter by letter together as a group.

- "Let's all stretch the word *sun.* Stretch the sounds with me. *s-s-s-s-s-u-u-u-u-n-n-n-n.* How many sounds did you hear? Yes, I heard three sounds too.
- Let's listen for the **first** sound. *s-s-s-s-s.* What did you hear? Yes, I heard the sound /s/. Put the letter *s* down **first**.

- Now let's stretch again. *s-s-s-s-u-u-u-u*. What sound do you hear **next**? Yes, I hear /u/. Put the letter *u* down **next**.
- Let's stretch it one more time *s-s-s-s-u-u-u-n-n-n-n-n-n*. What do you hear **last**? Yes, I hear /n/. Put an *n* down **last**."

Now, examine the word together letter by letter and sound by sound. Have your readers read the word slowly and touch or move each letter slightly as they read the word. You want them to coordinate their eyes, their mouth, and their finger. Watch each child individually and model, guide, or prompt them as needed.

Writing

Writing will continue to evolve over the course of working with Level C texts. Most children at this level jump at the opportunity to take on more responsibility as a writer. They begin to manage space on the paper, with correct left-to-right directionality, using appropriate letter size and good spacing between words on their own. They are also learning more and more high frequency words and how to break words apart, sound by sound, at a faster pace. As children become more confident in their writing abilities, they tend to become impatient about having to wait for everyone to finish a word before moving on to writing the next word . . . this is their way of saying, "I'm ready to try it on my own!" This new writing energy is a good thing and you will want to foster it and encourage it! Remember, our goal as teachers is to gradually release learning responsibility into the hands of the children. The tough part for you will be learning how to proficiently manage and support this for each individual child. Luckily, we can give you a few tips!

Before Writing

As you did in Levels A and B, you will want to craft a "story" about the book ahead of time because you want to maximize your teaching opportunities during the small group lesson. Since writing stamina is being built alongside becoming more fluent with linking sounds, writing letters, and high frequency words, the stories you craft while reading Level C texts will gradually get longer. Depending on your small group's ability, you might even want to consider crafting a story with two sentences.

As you craft the story, the questions we asked you to consider from Chapter 4 still apply through Level C. At Level C, there are many more possibilities to choose from, so Mrs. Jones must look critically at what E.J., Aubrey, TaShawn, and Deedra need to learn next. When she planned for her group to read the book *My Big Car* (Figure 5.17), she decided to:

1. Use the sentences *I see a box. I am going to make a big car.* because the children will be able to write the words *I, see, a, am, go,* and *to* quickly and fluently.
2. Use sound boxes for *box* or *big* or both, depending on what each child wants to attempt on their own.
3. Teach the word *going* because the children know *go* and are starting to notice inflectional endings as they read.
4. Watch each child closely to know what letter or high frequency word each one needs to practice due to lapses.

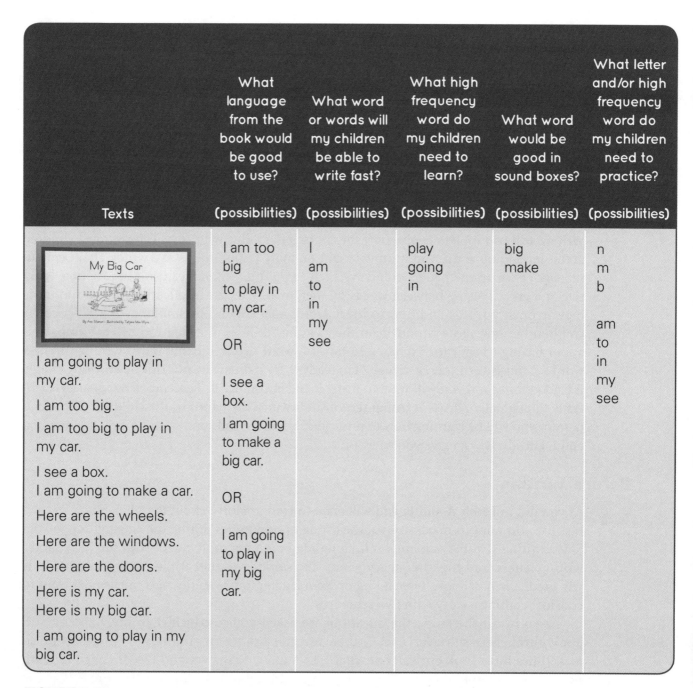

Texts	What language from the book would be good to use? (possibilities)	What word or words will my children be able to write fast? (possibilities)	What high frequency word do my children need to learn? (possibilities)	What word would be good in sound boxes? (possibilities)	What letter and/or high frequency word do my children need to practice? (possibilities)
My Big Car I am going to play in my car. I am too big. I am too big to play in my car. I see a box. I am going to make a car. Here are the wheels. Here are the windows. Here are the doors. Here is my car. Here is my big car. I am going to play in my big car.	I am too big to play in my car. OR I see a box. I am going to make a big car. OR I am going to play in my big car.	I am to in my see	play going in	big make	n m b am to in my see

FIGURE 5.17
Teaching Opportunities During Writing

During Writing

Don't forget to have that brief conversation about the story before you dictate the sentence! We can't stress enough the importance of talking about the story meaning—after all, it's the whole reason we read! Afterward you can dictate the "story" to the children, have them repeat it, count how many words they will write, and begin to write.

Early in Level C, the writing may still look and feel like the late lessons in Level B. You will continue to:

- Model the writing on the white board.
- Prompt for where children will begin their writing as well as how to organize the size of letters and space on the page.
- Keep children together as they write the "story."
- Prompt for fast responding to known letters and words.
- Select the new high frequency words to be learned.
- Choose the word(s) to explore in sound boxes.
- Prompt for rereading the story to know which word will come next.
- Prompt for punctuation.

Later in Level C, as students gain writing confidence, you'll notice children:

- Have stopped attending to what you are doing on the white board because they have turned their attention to their own writing. This is the time to set them free, no need to model anymore.
- Automatically starting their writing at the top left of the page and using correct directionality with a return sweep to the left when necessary.
- Self-starting their writing.
- Beginning their sentences with a capital letter and transitioning to using lowercase letters the rest of the time.
- Managing letter size and space on the page.
- Rereading their "story" independently before they write the next word.
- Responding fast when they write letters and words.
- Learning new high frequency words quickly.
- Using sound boxes efficiently from the beginning sound of the word through to the end sound and eventually not needing sound boxes for CVC words.
- Automatically adding a punctuation mark often at the end of each line. This makes for a great teaching point about the purpose of punctuation and which punctuation mark to use.

CHAPTER 5

FIGURE 5.18
Writing Transitions in Level C

Bear in mind, Level C is one of big transitions and expectations not only in reading but also in writing. Writers enter Level C dependent on your constant writing support. They leave Level C wanting some independence to try on their own! Figure 5.18 spells out many of these transitions that will take place over the course of Level C.

The most important transition you will see in writing around this level is from children who are ready for some independence and want to try the story on their own. As you try to keep them writing all together, it will probably seem as if this portion of the lesson becomes a little frantic. So, to alleviate that difficulty, we encourage you to take advantage of it and, instead, use it as an opportunity to step back a little. Here, when your students show you some of them are ready, let them start out writing the story on their own and then, based on what you observe, individualize the learning for students who still need your support. As these individual needs become more and more apparent, you'll be ready to individualize management of space, letter formation practice, high frequency word practice, and how much support students need with sound boxes.

After Writing

By the end of Level C, children will most likely finish their writing at different times. The first habit they should get into is rereading what they wrote, because children need to learn to monitor their writing for errors just as they monitor their reading. Asking students to reflect on their writing will help you consider goal(s) you might focus on in the next small group lesson. If time permits, let the children do a quick sketch of their story. This will help them to remember what they wrote when they come back to reread their own writing.

Remember to check out our correlating literacy center ideas that support the work students are doing at the small-group table with Level C texts.
www.stenhouse.com/content/intentional-from-the-start

REMEMBER THE PURPOSE OF TEACHING WITH LEVEL C TEXTS

Monitoring yourself doing any complex task is not easy. If it were, the car industry wouldn't have needed to develop cars that flash and beep at you when you stray from your lane. Even very experienced drivers are not perfect at monitoring their driving. We need to remember this as we teach young readers who are first learning how to check themselves and monitor their attempts at reading unpatterned books. It is so tempting to try to move these readers into solving every new word they encounter before they have firmed up their ability to monitor. Level C books give readers the perfect setting for learning to monitor what they know and then begin to solve new words, using the sources of information available to them. At first, as the teacher, you may have to flash and beep at them to help them stay in their lane, but very soon, they will be finding and correcting their own errors!

EXAMPLE LESSON WITH LEVEL C TEXT

Mrs. Jones has recently moved E.J. and Aubrey into a group with Deedra and TaShawn. Here, they've come together to read *Little Mouse*. This story is about a little mouse who is exploring in a pet shop and looks at many different animals in cages. At the end of the book, he quickly points out that he is not in a cage and runs back to his mouse hole. Over the course of the two days of lessons, Mrs. Jones will have the children:

- Read familiar books.
- Read the new book *Little Mouse*.
- Practice writing the high frequency words *see* and *am* quickly.
- Learn the new high frequency word *look*.
- Use sound boxes to decode CVC words.
- Discuss the book before writing about the little mouse. Mrs. Jones has several possibilities for what they could write about in mind and will decide based on the conversation and student interest.

Figure 5.19 is a glimpse into what it sounds like and looks like at Mrs. Jones's small group table during each of the different components of a Level C lesson.

DAY 1

Component: Familiar Reading
Focus: Phrased and fluent reading; monitoring with high frequency words

Mrs. Jones lays a selection of books from previous small group lessons on the table for children to reread: *A Turtle in the Sun; My Five Senses; Blue; The Cave; Going By*. As children read, Mrs. Jones listens in to each child. Depending on the errors children are making, she might prompt for:

- Shoring up momentary lapses in one-to-one matching.
- Monitoring known words.
- Using pictures to help solve unknown words.
- Using the first letter of a word to attempt to solve unknown words.
- More fluent reading.

As the others read, she takes a moment to check in on how things are going with Deedra.

Student and Teacher Interactions	**Teacher Moves and Rationale**
Deedra (reading *My Five Senses*): Here is my mouth. I can taste with my mouth.	Mrs. Jones leans in and listens to Deedra read *My Five Senses*.

FIGURE 5.19
Example Lesson for Little Mouse

Mrs. Jones: Hmmm, Deedra, something didn't look right. What would you expect to see at the beginning of the word *mouth*?

Deedra: /mmmmm/, *m*!

Mrs. Jones: Okay, let's check to see if it's mouth. What letter do you see?

Deedra: *t*.

Mrs. Jones: So, can it be *mouth*?

Deedra: No.

Mrs. Jones: Why not?

Deedra: Because *t* says /t/.

Mrs. Jones: Right! So, what begins with /t/ that would make sense? Here is my /t/ /t/ /t/ . . .

Deedra: *tongue*!

Mrs. Jones: Yes! Read that page again and see if *tongue* makes sense.

Deedra: Here is my tongue. I can taste with my tongue.

Mrs. Jones: That makes sense! Keep reading Deedra.

She wants to draw Deedra's attention to the first letter of *tongue* since she substituted *mouth*. She covers up all but the *t* in tongue.

After reading with Deedra, Mrs. Jones continues to check in with the other readers in the group individually before moving on to the next portion of the lesson.

Component: Introduce and Read the New Book: *Little Mouse*

Focuses: Monitoring known high frequency words; using the first letter and pictures to attempt to solve unknown words.

Time: 8–10 minutes

Student and Teacher Interactions

Mrs. Jones: Today we are going to read a book called *Little Mouse*. In this story, Little Mouse is running around a pet shop looking at all the animals. What animals do you think he might see?

E.J.: A dog! I got my dog from a pet store.

Mrs. Jones: You're right! He might see a dog.

TaShawn: A cat!

Aubrey: A turtle!

Mrs. Jones: I go to the pet store all the time and I always see cats and turtles. You may be right, TaShawn and Aubrey.

Deedra: Maybe a rabbit?

Teacher Moves and Rationale

Mrs. Jones shows the cover of the book *Little Mouse* to the children at her small group table. She chooses not to pass out individual copies right away because she wants everyone to focus on her copy for the book preview.

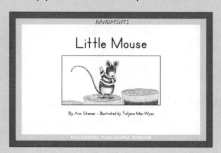

FIGURE 5.19   (*Continued*)

Mrs. Jones stagger starts the children reading by handing out books one at a time. She makes sure each child gets off to a good start and then listens in to each child as they whisper read the book to themselves. She zeros in on Aubrey when she notices Aubrey is stuck on the word *not*.

Student and Teacher Interactions	Teacher Moves and Rationale
Aubrey: I am (pauses, looks at the picture, back to the words, and then looks at Mrs. Jones). **Mrs. Jones:** What sounds do you see that can help you? **Aubrey:** /nnnn//ooo//t/, *not*! I am not in a cage! **Mrs. Jones:** Great job figuring that out Aubrey, now read it again.	Mrs. Jones prompts Aubrey to use letter sounds to solve the word *not* when checking the picture did not provide any information to her. Mrs. Jones continues to listen, prompt, and teach as everyone reads then shifts the group's focus to high frequency words.

Component: High Frequency Words: Fluency Practice and Learn a New Word
Focus: Learn the word *look*

Mrs. Jones has the children practice writing the known words *see* and *the* on their white boards to build their automaticity. Once finished, she teaches the new word *look*.

Student and Teacher Interactions	Teacher Moves and Rationale
Mrs. Jones: Let's learn a new word. The word *look* was in the book *Little Mouse* on almost every page. It is going to pop up in a lot of the books we will be reading, so we need to learn it. **Mrs. Jones:** Put your finger on your nose if you can find the word *lllllloooooook* on this page. (Mrs. Jones waits until everyone has their finger on their nose.) Tell me the letters in the word *look*. **Children:** *l, o, o, k*!	To ground this lifted word learning in authentic reading, Mrs. Jones goes back into the text to locate the new word *look*.
Mrs. Jones: Watch me make the word on my white board. What letter will I grab first? **Children:** *l*	To highlight that words are built left to right, Mrs. Jones slides the letter *l* down on the left side of the board . . .

FIGURE 5.19   (*Continued*)

Mrs. Jones: Yes! Look begins with *l* and you can hear that sound. Listen, /lllll/ook. What letter do I need to grab next? **Children**: *o, o* **Mrs. Jones:** That's right, *o, o* comes next. What is the last letter in *look*? **Children**: *k*! **Mrs. Jones:** *K* is the last letter in the word *look* and you can hear that sound. Listen, *loo/k/*. What word did I make? **Group:** *Look*!	. . . then she slides the two *o*'s into place. Finally, Mrs. Jones slides the *k* into position at the end of the word.
Mrs. Jones: Let's read it together. **Children:** *Look.*	Mrs. Jones slides her finger from left to right under the word *look* with precision.
Mrs. Jones: Now I want you to make the word *look* on your board	Mrs. Jones gives everyone the magnetic letters to build the work *look*.
Mrs. Jones: Aubrey, what word did you make? **Aubrey:** *Look*! (Reads it with her finger and eyes.) **Mrs. Jones:** (Mixes up the letters.) Now make it again.	Mrs. Jones watches as children make the word *look* on their boards several times. She's watching to make sure they build it correctly from left to right and then checking it with their finger and their eyes.
Mrs. Jones: Now I want you to write the word *look*. Get a wipe-off marker and write the word *look* on your board. **Mrs. Jones:** Deedra, take a good look at the word. I'm going to take the magnetic letters away. Can you write it? **Deedra:** Yes! (Deedra writes the word *look*.) **Mrs. Jones:** What word did you write Deedra? **Deedra:** *Look*! (Mrs. Jones erases the word.) **Mrs. Jones**: Write it again. **Mrs. Jones:** Open your book to your favorite page. Can you find the word *look*? **Children:** (Children search and point to the word *look*.) Right there!	As children finish writing the word *look* on their board Mrs. Jones asks them what word they wrote and erases it and removes the magnetic letters. She wants them to think about the word and letter order every time they write it rather than copying a model. This rapid process of writing, reading, and erasing continues until everyone has written and read the word *look* three or four times.

FIGURE 5.19   *(Continued)*

DAY 1 (Continued)

Mrs. Jones: You found the word *look*, now read your page again and then put your book in your book box.
(Children each read their page and put their books away.)

Component: Word Study
Focus: Decoding CVC words

Mrs. Jones shows the children how their use of sound boxes in writing can also help them when decoding CVC words in reading. Using the known word *dog*, she models, on her large white board, the process of pushing one magnetic letter at a time into sound boxes as she says the sounds. She blends the sounds together and reads the word fast and then invites every child to practice with the word *dog* before moving on to trying this process with unknown CVC words.

Student and Teacher Interactions

Mrs. Jones: Now it's your turn to try a word on your own. (Mrs. Jones puts the letters to the word *nut* under the sound boxes and gives the board to Deedra.) Give it a try Deedra.

Deedra: /nnnn/ /oooo/ /t/, *not*.

Mrs. Jones: Remember, this letter *u* makes the /u/ sound. Give it another try.

Deedra: /nnnn/ /uuuu/ /t/, *nut*!

Mrs. Jones: There you go, perfect! Your turn TaShawn!
(Mrs. Jones continues by giving TaShawn, Aubrey, and E.J. the letters for the words *pin*, *fan*, and *vet*.)

Mrs. Jones: Everyone did a fabulous job reading new words in sound boxes. We'll practice again the next time we get together. Soon, you'll be able to read these short words without the sound boxes!

Teacher Moves and Rationale

Mrs. Jones has the children work on her big board but changes the word for each child. This allows them the opportunity to solve a different CVC word and to have the support of their peers if they need it.

As children gain more experience decoding CVC words, Mrs. Jones will provide opportunities to practice this skill in pairs and then individually.

CHAPTER 5

FIGURE 5.19   (*Continued*)

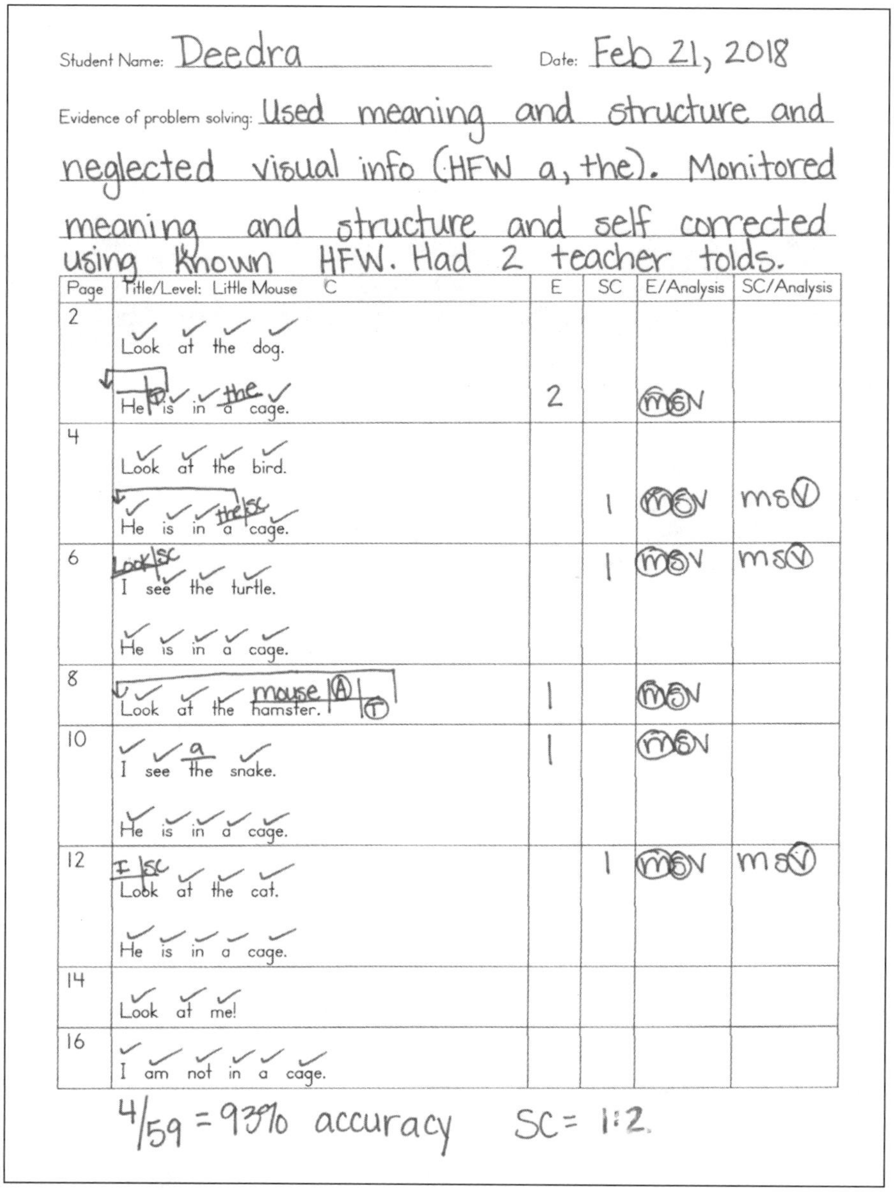

Student Name: Deedra Date: Feb 21, 2018

Evidence of problem solving: Used meaning and structure and neglected visual info (HFW a, the). Monitored meaning and structure and self corrected using known HFW. Had 2 teacher tolds.

Page	Title/Level: Little Mouse C	E	SC	E/Analysis	SC/Analysis
2	Look at the dog. He is in a cage.	2		MSV	
4	Look at the bird. He is in a cage.		1	MSV	msV
6	I see the turtle. He is in a cage.		1	MSV	msV
8	Look at the hamster.	1		MSV	
10	I see the snake. He is in a cage.	1		MSV	
12	Look at the cat. He is in a cage.		1	MSV	msV
14	Look at me!				
16	I am not in a cage.				

4/59 = 93% accuracy SC = 1:2.

CHAPTER 5

FIGURE 5.20

Deedra's Running Record for Little Mouse

Mrs. Jones has analyzed Deedra's running record. She notes that when Deedra read the *for* a *and* a *for* the, *she used meaning and structure but neglected using the print information. She didn't monitor using her known high frequency words. However, on three other errors, Deedra was able to monitor using high frequency words and self-correct those errors. Mrs. Jones knows it will be important to shore up Deedra's inconsistent monitoring of known high frequency words in text Level C. She chooses this to be her teaching point after a brief discussion about the story. Mrs. Jones was happy when Deedra read* mouse *for* hamster *and then appealed for assistance. This means Deedra noticed when something in the print information, most likely the first letter, didn't match what she was saying. Mrs. Jones knows she'll need to focus some instructional time on how to use meaning and print (letters and sounds) information to make reasonable attempts at solving these mismatches.*

DAY 2

Component: Reread Book from Day 1
Focus: Monitoring with known words; phrasing and fluency

Mrs. Jones invites Deedra, TaShawn, Aubrey, and E.J. back to the small group table for their Day 2 lesson using the book *Little Mouse*. While the children reread, Mrs. Jones takes a running record (see Figure 5.20 on previous page) of Deedra reading the story. This gives her insight into Deedra's strategic reading and gives her a sense of what Deedra can do independently.

Student and Teacher Interactions	Teacher Moves and Rationale
Deedra: Look at the dog. (Deedra pauses and looks at Mrs. Jones.) **Mrs. Jones:** He **Deedra:** He is in the cage. (Turns page.) Look at the bird. He is in the, a cage. (Turns page.) Look, I see the turtle. He is in the cage. (Turns page.) Look at the mouse. (Pauses and looks at Mrs. Jones.) Is it a mouse? **Mrs. Jones:** Hamster. **Deedra:** Oh! Look at the hamster. I see a snake. He is in a cage. (Turns page.) I, Look at the cat. He is in a cage. (Turns page.) Look at me. (Turns page.) I am not in the cage. (Closes book.)	When Deedra gets stuck and makes no attempt to problem solve or appeal for help, Mrs. Jones tells her the word. This allows Deedra to keep moving and not lose the story meaning. After Deedra finishes reading *Little Mouse*, Mrs. Jones has a quick conversation about the story before launching into her teaching points. This allows her to gauge Deedra's understanding of the story.
Mrs. Jones: (Turns to page 4.) When you read this page, you noticed when something didn't look right. (Points to the word *a*.) You said *the* but noticed it was . . . **Deedra:** *a!* **Mrs. Jones:** Right and because you were looking closely, you noticed it was a word you knew and you fixed it up! (Turns to page 10.) Read this page again because something didn't look right. Let's see if you can fix it up. Be sure to look closely!	Mrs. Jones carefully and quickly chooses her teaching point(s) after Deedra's reading. 1. On page 4, Deedra monitored and self-corrected using known words. She decides to celebrate with Deedra for noticing when something didn't look right and fixing her error. 2. On page 10, Deedra did not monitor for known words so Mrs. Jones directs her back to the page to try it again.

CHAPTER 5

FIGURE 5.19 (*Continued*)

DAY 2 (Continued)

Deedra: (Looking carefully.) I see the snake. He is in a cage.
Mrs. Jones: Did that look right?
Deedra: Yep!
Mrs. Jones: It sure did! Nice job looking closely and reading carefully!
Mrs. Jones: Alright everyone, put your books in your book boxes so you can enjoy it for the rest of the week.

Component: High Frequency Words: Fluency Practice; Review New Word from Day 1
Focus: Building automaticity with known and partially known words.

As a quick review, Mrs. Jones has everyone write the known high frequency words *see* and *am* on their own white boards. Then she has the children practice building the new high frequency word *look* with magnetic letters. This practice helps to secure their new learning from their previous lesson. As she watches them build the word *look* she notices E.J. builds it incorrectly and steps in to help him notice his error.

Mrs. Jones: E.J., what word did you build?
E.J.: (Builds *lkoo*.) *look*.
Mrs. Jones: Hmmm. Something doesn't look right at the end. Say that word slowly and run your finger under it. Think about the sound you hear at the end.
E.J.: /llllloooooook/.
Mrs. Jones: What sound do you hear at the end?
E.J.: /l/ /oo/ /k/, /k/ is at the end.
Mrs. Jones: Yes! So, what letter should you see at the end of your word?
E.J.: k!
Mrs. Jones: Right! Now try *look* again with your letters. (E.J. builds the word correctly on the whiteboard.) Are you right?
E.J.: /lllloooook/, yes! (Mrs. Jones mixes up the letters.)
Mrs. Jones: Good job making it look right E.J.! Now make the word *look* again.
(This process is repeated quickly, three or four times simultaneously with all the children.)

Mrs. Jones guides E.J. to notice the word *look* ends with the letter *k*. She helps him to focus on the sound first and then the letter.

Mrs. Jones knows this part of the lesson should be fast. The purpose is for children to gain automaticity with building and writing high frequency words so they can use their mental energy in other places.

Once they're finished practicing, Mrs. Jones has the children pull out *Little Mouse* again to locate and read the word *look* in the text before moving on to the writing portion of the lesson.

FIGURE 5.19 *(Continued)*

Component: Writing
Focus: Leaving spaces between words; writing high frequency words fast, using sound boxes to write sound regular words.

After a brief discussion about *Little Mouse*, Mrs. Jones decides the children will write the sentences: *Look at the snake. He is in the cage.* She dictates the sentence because she has specific goals for the children to work on during writing. She knows the children will be able to quickly write the high frequency words: *look, at, the, is, in.* She will use sound boxes to help the children write the word *snake*.

After having the children practice the word *look* on their practice page, Mrs. Jones allows the children to write at their own pace. She carefully monitors for when a child might need assistance or sound boxes drawn.

Student and Teacher Interactions

TaShawn: Look at the . . . snake. Mrs. Jones, how do you write snake?

Mrs. Jones: Let's use some sound boxes. Now touch one box for each sound you hear in *snake*.

TaShawn: /sn/ /a/ /k/

Mrs. Jones: That first part is a little tricky! Watch me as I do it. /s/ /n/ /a/ /k/. Now you try it.

TaShawn: /s/ /n/ /a/ /k/ (touches the sound boxes correctly for each sound)

Mrs. Jones: There you go TaShawn! You got it that time. Now write the letters you hear in the boxes. Be sure to start at the beginning box. E.J., read to me what you have written so far.

Teacher Moves and Rationale

Mrs. Jones draws four sound boxes in TaShawn's writing book.

TaShawn touches the same box for /sn/ so Mrs. Jones decides to model separating the sounds using the sound boxes. Mrs. Jones does not worry about the silent *e* at this time because her focus is on segmenting, hearing, and writing the letters he can hear. She knows there will be plenty of time in the future to learn about silent *e* once this skill is well developed.

Mrs. Jones continues to support her writers by offering assistance as needed until everyone is finished with their writing. She reminds E.J. to leave spaces between his words. She helps Deedra figure out if *cage* begins with a *c* or a *k* by providing her the picture link *cat* from the alphabet chart. She also encourages Aubrey to reread her writing to help her maintain meaning and know what to write next.

FIGURE 5.19

Learning How to Integrate Information in Print

Mrs. Jones knows it's time to shift her small reading groups once again. Throughout the year, she keeps her small groups fluid and moves children based on what they need to learn next or need more time practicing. Since all of her students can fluently name forty-eight or more upper- and lowercase letters she has abandoned the letter identification assessment. She continues to monitor those students who have visual confusions (b/d/p/q) and has those students practice those letters outside of the small group reading table. Running records continue to guide most of her instructional reading decisions. The other assessment Mrs. Jones finds extremely useful for aiding in making instructional decisions about writing is a dictated sentence. She discovered this assessment from Marie Clay's *Observation Survey (2005b)* and, through collaboration with her grade-level teammates, created a sentence to use with their students that is similar to Clay's assessment. The dictated sentence she uses is: *My monster has a big, shiny hat with a pink rose on it.*

The information Mrs. Jones gathers from this assessment is invaluable. She learns if children can:

➤ Say, hear (phonological awareness), link, and record letter sounds (phonics) in sequence when attempting unknown words (monster, big, shiny, hat, pink, rose).

➤ Write high frequency words correctly (My, has, a, with, on, it).

➤ Begin at the top of the page, write text from left to right, and use a return sweep if necessary.

➤ Leave spaces between words.

➤ Use punctuation.

➜

Mrs. Jones administers the dictated sentence assessment one on one or in small groups so she can observe carefully what children are doing as they write. First, she reads the entire sentence without stopping and then rereads it again one word at a time, so the students can write it. She takes notes if necessary, so she can transfer them onto the student's paper when she scores the assessment. Figure 6.1 shows Johnny's dictated sentence. along with Mrs. Jones's notes and her scoring.

Johnny controls:

- top-to-bottom directionality;
- left-to-right directionality;
- return sweep on two lines of text.

Johnny can:

- write the high frequency words: my, a, on;
- hear, link, and record sounds in sequence: monster, has, big, shiny, hat, with, pink, rose, it.

Johnny needs instruction on:

- word spacing;
- learning new high frequency words;
- how to hear, link, and record all sounds in sequence when writing longer words;
- building his bank of high frequency words in writing.

FIGURE 6.1

Once Mrs. Jones has scored the assessment, she looks for common themes, both on running records and the dictated sentence, to aid in readjusting her instructional small groups. Aubrey and E.J. continue to make similar progress. They understand how print works both in books and when writing. In writing, they are proficient using letters and sounds to compose readable texts using both high frequency words and kid-spelled words. This proficiency in writing is beginning to transfer over to reading. Along with using meaning and structure, Aubrey and E.J. are taking the initiative to use the letters and sounds they see in unknown words to attempt solving and decoding those words. Their reading and writing vocabularies are growing quickly now that they have a system in place for learning and remembering high frequency words. Aubrey and E.J. are ready to attempt some easy Level D books in their small group.

Karie and Johnny both need more instruction and experience with how print works. In books, they understand that print moves from top to bottom and left to right, with return sweeps to the left. However, in writing, when they have to manage the space on a blank page themselves, this knowledge is *known with lapses.* They need to become proficient at leaving spaces between their words every time they write. Karie and Johnny have a small base of known words both in reading and writing so they need to grow both of these vocabularies. In reading, both children are monitoring using known high frequency words. They are also using pictures and the first letter sounds to attempt to problem solve unknown words. Without teacher prompting, neither are looking and decoding across a word to check their solving attempts yet. Another book or two in harder Level C texts would likely firm up learning for Karie and Johnny.

From gathering and analyzing information about all of her students as readers and writers, Mrs. Jones knows some of her children are ready to attempt some easy Level D books. She is cautious because she knows moving into text Level D can be a big jump and might cause some apprehension in her beginning readers, but she is ready to provide appropriate support so her children experience success when the new learning feels hard.

E.J. and Aubrey are ready to try the new challenges in text Level D. So, what does that look like? Let's begin by reviewing what our readers will have firmly in place as Level C books begin to feel easy and look at what they'll be ready to take on in the more complex text of Level D and beyond. See Figure 6.2.

It's time to take those floaties off our swimmers' arms and let them swim. They now have the skills they need to move themselves across the water. These young swimmers are ready to fluidly integrate the skills they practiced so carefully before. Once the floaties come off, swimmers immediately notice that they can no longer concentrate on only one skill at a time. Just kicking their feet but not moving their arms doesn't get them very far. They need to coordinate their arms and legs together, in a fluid, forward movement to gain the momentum they need to get across the water. Our readers will need to do the same thing. Once they are reading Level D and beyond, paying attention to just one source of information at a time won't keep them afloat. We will expect their eyes to check the print first, their mouths to begin to voice the sounds, while they simultaneously think about meaning. They will need to integrate multiple skills fluidly and Level D books give readers the perfect practice space for this.

CHAPTER 6

What does the child know and control?	What is the child ready to learn?
■ Enjoys listening to picture books being read aloud ■ Makes connections and loves to talk when listening to a book ■ Knows readers turn the pages of a book ■ With support, can tell an oral story that has a beginning, middle, and end ■ Can draw a simple story and is beginning to use a variety of colors ■ Usually can write their first name ■ Knows print contains the message ■ Can locate their name in print ■ Left-to-right directionality across one line of text ■ One-to-one voice-to-print matching ■ Letter names and sounds ■ Return sweep back to the left on two or more lines of text ■ How to use initial letter and sound to solve unknown words ■ How to use the initial letter and sound to monitor attempts at unknown words	■ More high frequency words at a faster pace ■ Monitoring using a larger core of known high frequency words ■ Looking across a word to attempt to solve it ■ Begin to use analogies to read and write new words ■ Begin to integrate meaning, structure, and letter and sound information when attempting to solve unknown words ■ Hearing sounds in sequence on more complex words in writing ■ Solving CVC words quickly ■ Reading more fluently with a focus on phrasing ■ Using sound boxes for more complex words

FIGURE 6.2

Learners Who Are Ready for Level D Texts

MY CHILDREN ARE MONITORING AND ATTEMPTING TO SOLVE. NOW WHAT?

Some heavy lifting was accomplished with Level C texts. Readers learned to check their reading with some visual monitoring and they began to use a bit of print information to solve new words. This is huge! Many children for the first time feel like they are "really" reading, and they are eager to add even more skills to their repertoire. Complexity in syntax, story line, and, especially, print information will increase as we head into Level D, so let's take a look at the skills children will need to develop even further.

Breaking Words into Parts to Solve

In the books our children have been reading so far, using known high frequency words and the first letter of words has served them well enough. This was fine in their earliest learning about how to match voice to print and how to look at first letters first, as they articulated first sounds. All that is quite a bit to juggle for print novices, but now it's time to build on those experiences and move on. So far, in writing, these same readers have had lots of practice in sound boxes, hearing sounds in order, and matching letters to those sounds, across whole words. Now, we'll be asking them to use these skills in reading, to solve new words in the books they read.

At times, readers will find it most efficient to approach words letter by letter, sound by sound, as they do in writing in sound boxes. Sometimes, it will be more efficient to approach words by clusters of letters, and chunks of sounds, for faster solving. Readers need to make decisions about which approach might be most efficient for them at a particular time and must be flexible in strategic solving. We will start exposing children to these concepts in Level D, as we look at digraphs, consonant clusters, and syllables. We will show children how to break words into onset and rime and how to break syllables to help them attempt to solve unknown words in print.

Using Meaning and Print Information Together to Solve Words in Text

Sometimes in early levels, our running records might reveal readers who just used one source of information to attempt a word they didn't know. This is normal, expected, and just fine—in the earliest levels. Now, however, we don't want readers who only do one thing. Just as we never see swimmers forgetting to kick their feet, we shouldn't see readers forgetting to use the print or forgetting to think about meaning. Effective readers hold onto meaning as they decode. We call errors that make sense and look visually similar to the correct word "integrated errors" and if you're going to make an error, this is the best kind to make! For example, if a child reads *house* for *home*, they have likely considered both meaning and the beginning letters. Your future teaching can help them look beyond those first letters, but for now, you know they are considering several sources of information as they read.

Reading With Phrasing

Fluency has certainly become a hot topic in the last decade and has often become synonymous with words per minute. We know rate is just one component of fluency, although it's the component that seems to get all the attention. We are going to focus, however, on phrasing. Phrasing involves both the eyes and the ears. The reader has to be able to see which groups of words to read together before pausing and has to be able to hear which groups of words sound right together. Phrasing is a meaning-making and meaning-monitoring skill. Thanks to smart publishers, many Level D texts are written with easy-to-see and easy-to-hear phrases. These books help children begin to navigate more complex syntax with careful scaffolding.

Learning About Long Vowel Sounds in Sound Boxes

As we've mentioned before, when teaching children about phonics, we lead with writing. Earlier, we introduced consonant-vowel-consonant words in sound boxes. We would now expect our readers to be able to solve these words in text. Meanwhile, as they begin applying their skills with CVC words to read text, we escalate the skills we are teaching with sound boxes in writing. At this point, we begin introducing long vowels in sound boxes. This would include words with *silent e* or *vowel teams*. At the same time, our short vowel words also become more complex, with digraphs, consonant clusters, and some two-syllable words.

KEY CHARACTERISTICS OF LEVEL D TEXTS

You may have already been dipping into your Level D baskets as your readers have become more accomplished with Level C books. In fact, that's how it should be, with children dipping in and out of a variety of similar text levels. We choose our books for instruction based on what opportunities we need at the time. But in general, when your children are firmly ready to leave most Level C books behind, you will have certain text characteristics in mind and Level D will provide many of the challenges your readers need. Level D books kick everything up a notch. Everything is longer—the storylines, the sentences, and the words. Think about the following text characteristics as you shop in your Level D baskets.

- The text pages should mostly have multiple lines of print. Often, the sentences will be long enough to need more than one line of print, requiring the reader to hold the meaning and the syntax in mind as they return sweep (just as you did right now!)
- The sentences in these books will often contain prepositional phrases, sometimes laid out by line, to be easier to notice visually.
- The stories will contain more dialogue, often with more than one speaker. This means punctuation will play a larger role in these books as well.
- Children will need opportunities to solve new words in context, so these books should have multiple chances to solve simple words. Make sure the reader will actually have to use the print and won't be able to just use the picture to figure out unknown words at this level.
- High frequency words continue to play an important role in early reading, so quality Level D books should continue to increase a reader's exposure to the most common high frequency words. You'll want your readers to become faster and more automatic with the words they already know and continue adding to their bank of known words.

You probably remember the important milestone moments in Level C. It was so exciting to see readers monitoring less patterned text and using some anchors in print, such as high frequency words and first letters of words. In Level D books, we're going to watch for readers who can solve new words in context by breaking them into parts and using meaning as a check. These readers will read groups of words together in meaningful phrases. And when we check our running records, most errors should show them integrating more than one source of information in their attempts. When we see these behaviors consistently, we'll know students are navigating Level D texts successfully.

TEACHING WITH LEVEL D TEXTS

One of our purposes for writing this book was to provide support for teachers using the earliest levels of books. The most well-known, common instructional procedures used in guided reading don't always work so well with our earliest readers, in these earliest of levels. By the time your children are reading Level D books, however, they are no longer print newbies and they are becoming old hats at small group reading. The procedures we discuss in this chapter will likely seem more familiar, because they're more like procedures you use when teaching with your higher-level books.

Small group routines will now be in full swing. The children are learning to listen strategically to book introductions and becoming better at navigating these little books on their own. The routines for learning high frequency words, learning about breaking and changing words, and writing about their reading are feeling comfortable. This is critical as the texts they read and write become even more complex. We'll continue to follow the same lesson formats we used with Level C books (Figure 6.3), but as always, you as the teacher will adapt as needed to meet the needs of the children sitting before you.

Day 1	Day 2	Optional Day 3
Familiar Reading	Reread New Book from Day 1	Reread Familiar Books
New Book: ■ Teacher introduces the book. ■ Students whisper read or partner read.	High Frequency Words: ■ Fluency Practice ■ Review New Word from Day 1	High Frequency Words: ■ Review Words ■ Assess words as needed
High Frequency Words: ■ Fluency Practice ■ Learn a New Word		
Word Study (phonemic awareness and phonetic development)	Writing	Word Study (phonemic awareness and phonetic development)

FIGURE 6.3
Text Level C Lesson Cycle

Introducing the New Book

As we mentioned earlier, at this point, you probably won't need to use the special adaptations we suggested for introducing books at Levels A to C. Book introductions will now become more similar to the introductions you'll use in higher-level books. The procedures we outline below will not be specific to just Level D (Figure 6.4). If you can successfully introduce a Level D book, you've got the skills to introduce books in Levels E, F, G, and beyond!

As an example, let's look at *No, Bo!*, a Level D book about a dog named Bo, who climbs up on different pieces of furniture each day of the week. Although the opening sentence structure is the same on each page, we see the typical Level D increase in complexity: prepositional phrases, dialogue, changes in sentence structure, multisyllable words, and multiple lines of print. The book provides lots of opportunities for word work, with words that contain digraphs, consonant clusters, inflectional endings, and multisyllable words.

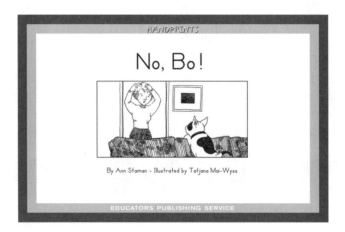

FIGURE 6.4
No, Bo!, *Cover*

Big Idea

Give a quick heads-up about what this story will be about, with perhaps a hint about how the story will work if necessary. Your children will most likely pipe in with their thoughts about the cover picture and title. The cover picture indicates that the boy is not happy with Bo being on the furniture, as does the title, so this is a great opportunity to model making inferences. In our example, the book is a days-of-the-week book, so you might want to casually mention that. This can all be done in a very short time!

You might say:

> Here is your new book, *No, Bo!* This dog is Bo and he likes to get on furniture. Why do you think it might be called *No, Bo!*? (wait for student responses). Yes, I bet you're right! That's why the boy looks so upset and I bet he's the one saying, "No, Bo!" As we read this book, you'll notice that each page happens on a different day of the week, so let's take a look at that now.

Meaning and Language Structure

You now have decisions to make. How much of the language of the story do you want to plant in their ear? How much do you want to leave for them to solve? As the professional, you will make a different decision each time you use each book, because you will be teaching a different group of readers. But in general, you can think about a few things. Well-written

Level D books should not be so patterned that each page repeats the same language pattern. You shouldn't need to worry too much about revealing sentence structures, since they will hopefully change somewhat on each page, so it's unlikely that a child will be able to memorize exactly what you say for each page. If there is tricky or complicated language, you may want to casually use that language in your introduction. Hearing unfamiliar language once will make it sound right as they process the print for themselves later. In our example, you might want them to hear the phrase "On Monday," because the phrases with the days of the week will play such an important role and most of the pages begin with the day of the week. It's always a good idea to establish supports that help children be successful with the very first words in a book, so they can open to the first page and feel confident in getting started with reading it.

You might say:

> Let's see what Bo did on Monday. Oh dear, he climbed up on the chair! And Mom is not happy about it! Do you see the words that say, "On Monday"? Put your finger under them and read them. Good!

Continue guiding the children through the book. You may decide to stop and talk about every page, but likely you won't need to. One big decision you'll make is whether you want to reveal the ending during the book introduction or let your readers discover it for themselves. If at all possible, it's nice, as a reader, to discover endings for yourself. However, there are times when the last page holds tricky language or tricky words that you anticipate will be impossible to navigate without support. For these books, you'll probably want to visit the ending together during the book introduction, which is just fine. It can be fun to be surprised at an ending together during the introduction too!

Letters and Sounds Information

As you have in previous levels, you'll have chosen a few words to pause and examine closely as you're moving through the book. Thinking about our goals for readers taking on Level D books, you'll want to choose words that match the skills you're teaching. For our example in *No, Bo!* on page 3 (Figure 6.5), you might decide to call attention to a digraph, a consonant cluster, and a multisyllable word. That would be enough for the whole book. We don't want to get crazy looking at too many words and we don't want our introduction to take too much time! Below is an example of what you could say and invite children to do as you prepare them to use their knowledge of letters, letter clusters, and words to solve an unfamiliar multisyllable word in print.

Concluding Statement

Decide on which page you'll end your introduction. Are you going to save the ending for readers to discover on their own? Or are you going to experience the ending together as a group? Are you going to ask for predictions right before you all turn the last page? Make these decisions ahead of time. Then once your introduction is over and you are ready to send your readers off to enjoy the book, you may want to give a brief reminder about the book's big idea and quick reminder about what new skill they may want to use to solve any tricky words.

On Monday,
Bo climbed up on the chair.

"No!" shouted Mom.
"Get down!"

multisyllable word: Monday

This page happens on Monday. Let's see if we can find the word Monday *and take a closer look at it. First, let's clap it and listen for how many syllables it has . . . Mon . . . day . . . Great, that's two syllables. See if you can find the word* Monday. *Now, let's look for those two syllables . . . Mon . . . day. Cover the ending with your finger, so all you see is* Mon. (Check the children to see if they can isolate the part that says Mon.) *Now show yourself the last part,* day. *Now read the whole word,* Monday!

FIGURE 6.5
No, Bo! *Pages 2 and 3*

You might say:

> You're ready to read about Bo climbing on the furniture every day! Remember, you know how to break words into parts to figure them out if you need to. Let's read about Bo!

Reading the New Book

The first pages of books are sometimes the hardest, so make sure everyone has a good start before leaning in to listen carefully to individuals. Have your dry erase board ready for quick prompting and demonstrating if needed. As you listen to each child, here are some suggestions for how to scaffold at Level D.

Teaching and Prompting During Reading

Some of the biggest shifts your readers will encounter as they move into Level D texts and beyond are the number and complexity of unknown words they encounter. They will need to have flexible plans for what to do when they come to words they don't know. They need to understand that they aren't expected to *know* all the words and just making the first sound won't be enough now to figure out unknown words, as it often was in the earliest levels. No one single strategy will work for all the complex words they will encounter in the myriad of complex sentence structures they will read. So, the students' goal for these first lessons is to stay ready to try more than one thing—a good lesson for problem solving in general!

Breaking Unfamiliar Words into Parts

Solving words in text needs to be done quickly to maintain meaning. The child's first plan should be to start the word without taking their eyes off the print. If the word is a simple CVC word, at this point, your readers will likely be able to smoothly blend the sounds, read the word, and keep going. If the word is slightly more complex, it may help to look at the word in parts. The word work you have been doing all along with magnetic letters has been good practice for this. Your readers have been making words, moving the first letter to the left, and then moving it back in place. This explicit breaking of words is good preparation for the efficient decoding that needs to happen as readers solve words quickly in text. Now, they need to explore looking at larger parts of words, or clusters of letters, as this can be a more efficient way to decode.

You have scaffolding decisions to make whenever a reader hesitates at an unknown word. If your goal is for the reader to say the word in parts, you'll need to decide how much support they need. Do they need you to model the process explicitly? Should you share the task? Or will a verbal prompt be enough? This will depend of course on the child, the word, and the context. Keep in mind, if you start with a prompt and it's not enough, you can always move toward more support. Let's look at a few examples of different ways to encourage children to say words in parts. Then we'll look specifically at some helpful types of word parts that come up frequently in Level D books.

- Model explicitly—If the word part you want the child to notice is new or if you have tried a less-supportive scaffold without success, you may want to explicitly show the child how to see, say, and blend the word parts.

  1. Make the word easier to see by writing it on the whiteboard. See Figure 6.6. Underline the focus letters that you want the child to notice. Articulate the word in parts, running your finger under the word parts as you say them. Then read the word as a whole. You may also want to use magnetic letters if you can access them quickly enough.

FIGURE 6.6
Shouted *Modeled Explicitly on the Teacher's White Board*

2. Invite the student to try saying the word in parts, running their finger under the word on the white board.

3. Say, "Now put it back in the story. Start here." Point to the beginning of the sentence, so the word will be in context when the child has to recode it.

- Share the task
  If the child has a bit of experience with the type of word part you are hoping they will use, you may want to offer just a medium amount of support. You may not want to model saying the parts of the word for them and instead help them see the parts of the word for themself. Some options for scaffolding include:
  - Using a small paper mask (see Figure 6.7) to show the word parts you want the reader to say, from left to right.
  - Writing the word parts on the white board, part by part, as they say them. Then point for them to read from the beginning of the sentence.

FIGURE 6.7
A teacher slides a word mask across the word Thursday *to highlight its parts.*

- Prompt
  If you think the child just needs a reminder to use what they know, give them as much independence as possible, by prompting. Even your prompts allow you to customize how much support to give. Will you give just a general reminder to take action or will you tell them specifically which information to use? Here are some sample prompts, from least supportive to most supportive.
  - "Try something."
  - "What do you know about that word?"
  - "Where will you break it?"

- "Break it before the vowel."
- "Say the part you know (*big*), now add the /*er*/."

In Level D text, readers will encounter a wider array of words, making the stories more interesting. Choose carefully which words you ask children to break apart as they begin to learn more complex decoding skills. Up to this point, they have good experience with letter-by-letter breaking of CVC patterns. Now, let's look at four types of letter clusters you'll want to teach your readers to notice and use as they decode more complex unfamiliar words in text. This will increase their efficiency in decoding longer, more complex words.

Digraphs and Consonant Blends

Digraphs are combinations of two letters representing one sound. Examples include *th*, *sh*, *ch*, *wh*, and *ph*. Children reading Level D books will be familiar with high frequency words that have some digraphs. Words such as *the*, *she*, and *where* can be used as links to remind children of the sound represented by common digraphs. You may keep an anchor chart handy as well to help children see these first at the beginning of words, where they are easiest to see, then at the end.

Consonant blends are combinations of two or three consonants whose sounds blend together, but each sound can still be heard. Examples include *br*, *bl*, *st*, *pl*, *pr*, *fl*, *spl*, and *str*. Children may be familiar with words like *play*, *stop*, *black*, *brown*, and *green*, which may help them understand the concept of a consonant blend. Look first for children to use these when they occur at the beginning of a word, but then help them see them embedded within a word, as in *coaster*.

Onset/Rime

The **onset** of a single-syllable word is the part that precedes the vowel. The **rime** is the rest of the single-syllable word, from the vowel on. Research indicates teaching children to use these parts of words has benefits for their reading development (Goswami and Bryant 1990). When children approach an unfamiliar word, we want them to look immediately for an onset to begin to articulate. Some words don't have an onset! That's when those flexible plans come into play and readers look for another plan of strategic action.

As children become familiar with a larger reading vocabulary, they will also become familiar with more and more common rimes. They will not need to approach these rimes with a letter-by-letter sounding strategy because they can get the word more quickly through analogy to other words with the same rime. You may call these "word families." Figure 6.8 is the word family chart that hangs in Carolyn's classroom and is referred to often in both reading and writing.

When helping children to use the rime in solving new words, at first you may need to show them the word they already know with the same rime. So, if they come to the word *hike*, you may want to write the word *like* with the word *hike* underneath it on the white board. Underline the rime in both words, articulating it for the child. You need to make it clear that the rimes sound the same in both words. The child only needs to change the first sound to read the new word. This skill requires early prerequisite skills of phonological awareness, so all your early work in that area is now ready to pay off in this more complex reading skill. Children will just be beginning to use this skill in their reading and writing, most likely in very simple words.

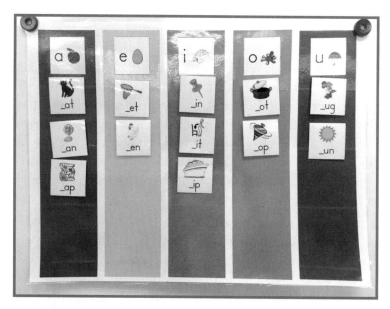

FIGURE 6.8
Common Word Families

Inflectional Endings

An **inflectional ending** is a letter or group of letters added to the end of a word that changes the word's meaning. At Level D, common endings include *–s*, *–ed*, *–ing*, and *–er*. Children will have been introduced to this concept in earlier levels but will see these endings more, on words they already know, as well as on new words in Level D. Look for easy-to-read words such as *looking*, more challenging words such as *shouted*, and even more challenging words like *roller coaster*, where all the parts are new.

Compound Words and Syllables

Our eventual goal is for our readers to be able to decode multisyllable words. An easier first step towards this goal is to recognize simple **compound words**, or two words put together to form a new word. Well-written leveled books will scatter a few of these words throughout, as early as Level C. Look for words such as *today, inside,* and *into*. These are easier because less decoding is really needed. Children will recognize both syllables and can spend their brain power learning how to look at two parts of a word and then say them together. The next step will be to decode simple, easy-to-decode, multisyllable words. Level D texts provide many opportunities to practice this skill. In *No, Bo!* we have a few perfect words for a beginner, such as *sister* and *Sunday*. You can reveal syllables to the child with a masking card, left to right, or you can write them on the white board, syllable by syllable.

Using Print Information and Meaning Together

If you consider the literacy journey your readers have traveled, most of them probably began as "inventors" of text, who looked at the pictures and made up a story. They were solely focused on meaning making. You've spent time in the early levels teaching them how print works and the beginnings of how to match their speech to the print. Now the complex juggling act of dual attention will bump things up a notch. We'll call on these young readers to pull together everything they know about print and letters and sounds to solve print. At the same time, however, we want them to use the text's meaning to (1) propel their solving, (2) monitor their attempts, and (3) provide the enjoyment that makes them love stories.

An early step in this complex process is **cross-checking** behavior. We called on our readers to cross-check in Level C if they read *frog* for *toad*. We would say "That makes sense, but what letter would you see at the beginning of *frog*?" We were acknowledging their use of meaning but asking them to consider the print. By the time they are proficient readers of Level C texts, we hope they can do this cross-checking on their own. By Level D, we expect rare cross-checking for first letters, because our readers should be more automatic at solving words with the beginning sounds. There will always be slip-ups, where the language a reader expects slips out or the meaning a reader expects overrides the print. (Don't you sometimes make a mistake as you read aloud to your class?) But we expect these errors to become infrequent and to be self-corrected.

Cross-checking was a sign the child was considering one source of information and then weighing it against another source. They now need to consider multiple sources of information at the same time to make the best decision as quickly as possible. This is referred to as integrating multiple sources of information.

You can encourage this shift away from cross-checking with your prompting where you work to balance the child's use of meaning and print—whichever source of information they are neglecting is the one you need to call their attention to. Some children who have just discovered print become very print focused and neglect meaning. You may hear them just making letter sounds, when simply rereading the sentence instead would help them make obvious sense. Others have a hard time giving up spontaneous, meaning-based attempts before they have checked the print. They need to always start with the print. This is why every child needs to have a knowledgeable teacher listen in to their reading!

Children tend to learn what we teach them. If your children tend to neglect one source of information, check yourself. You may lean too heavily toward prompting for one source of information. Try to make sure you let children know they should be considering both print and meaning. Here are some sample prompts to try.

- If the child is only considering meaning:
  - "That makes sense. Does it look right? Go back and when you get to the word, get ready for these sounds." (You might put magnetic letters on the board that helps the child to focus on the first letter, digraph, or blend. Or you might write letters on the white board.)
  - "You were thinking about what would make sense, and now go back and use the letters to make sure it looks and sounds right."
- If the child is only considering the letters and sounds:
  - "You're using the letters. Now go back and think about what would make sense."
  - If the child is using the letters inefficiently (letter by letter, when using a rime would help), show them the part that would help. "Try using this part of the word –*ike*. Now go back and read again and think about what would make sense."

Reading with Phrasing and Intonation

A lack of fluency can signal problems with other components of reading. So, we need to attend to fluency before it becomes a habituated problem. But it's a mistake to focus on words per minute when readers are working in Level D texts. These readers have just begun being careful examiners of print. Some still may actually need to slow down a bit to carefully check the print. However, all of them need to sound natural in their use of language when they read and then shore up speed when they're ready. Well-written Level D books support this learning. Clay (2005b) and Rasinski and Cheesman Smith (2018) described many ways to support readers in increasing fluency without just focusing on words per minute.

In addition to **rate**, or how fast a reader reads, fluency includes **phrasing**, which is the meaningful grouping of words together. This occurs naturally in speech. In reading, if a child is reading word by word, meaning can be distorted and no longer sound like natural language. We need to watch for this and help children use their *ears* to listen for what their reading sounds like and use their *eyes* to look for which words to group together. In many leveled books, the authors have laid out the print in phrases to make this easier for children.

On page 11 of *No, Bo*, Figure 6.9, we can see five distinct meaningful groups of words. This page would be a perfect page to practice putting together words that belong together. The time it takes the child to return their eyes to the left starting point of the next line is a nice pause in the reading, at just the right time. Children should not be using their pointing finger on this unless they come to a part where they feel they really need to look closely. Taking their finger out will allow that natural timing to happen that makes the reading sound like natural speech.

Dialogue is another easy place to help students increase their fluency. Prompting students to make it sound like the character would say it causes them to put words together and use **intonation**, or expression. **Intonation** is the way our voices change in tone, pitch, and volume when we talk. Dialogue will also expose readers to punctuation and give them more reasons to learn about what punctuation is telling them to do with their voice.

On Friday,

Bo climbed up

on my sister's bed.

She shouted,

"No, Bo! Get down!"

11

FIGURE 6.9
No, Bo!, *Page 11*

Here are some teaching strategies and prompts to help children read with phrasing and intonation.

- Mask the text to show the groups of words in phrases, unmasking as the child reads each phrase. You may need to model what it sounds like to put the words together. You read one phrase and let the child read the next. If you just have them echo you, you will not get a shift. It's easy to mimic what you hear. They need to be able to do this on print they read themselves.
- You can model what the dialogue should sound like. Then have the child read the dialogue on another page.
- Explicitly teach what to do when a reader encounters a comma, period, question mark, and exclamation mark.
- Mask phrases and prompt, "Read these words altogether."
- "Make it sound like they would say it."
- "Try that again and use the commas."
- "Make your voice go up for the question mark."

Whether we are focusing our teaching on breaking words, or integrating print and meaning, or reading fluently, the gradual release of responsibility model is always a great guide to keep in mind. We never want to give more support than a child needs, but we never want to withhold the modeling a child might need to understand a new strategy. It's not easy to always hit the mark just right. Remember, you can start with less support and then add more as needed. Figure 6.10 helps summarize what various levels of support might look like while teaching with Level D books.

Teaching Points After the Reading

When it's time to stop reading, give your readers their signal to come back together. Readers read at different rates. Some may have had time to reread some of the book while others may just be finishing. No matter how tight time feels, your most important teaching point will be to model the enjoyment of reading. Take the time to enjoy the book with your children. Get their genuine reactions. Laugh with them or marvel over any surprising parts. Then make a quick, memorable, focused teaching point. For example, in *No, Bo!* you might explore how the /sh/ in *she* and the familiar word *out* can help solve the word *shouted*. You might also take a close look at the punctuation and talk about what we do with our voices when we see a comma or an exclamation point.

Rereading Familiar Books

Day 2 and Day 3 lessons provide opportunities to reread previously read books. We've mentioned the benefits of reading familiar books before, but it's worth a quick repeat. Rereading books goes a little faster on subsequent readings, so this increases the amount of reading children do during the reading component of the lesson. Reading volume (amount, not sound!) matters in consolidating skills (Allington 2012), learning new words, and increasing automaticity. Just to review, we lay previously read books out on the table. On Day 2, children begin by rereading the new book from Day 1, but otherwise children can choose from any books on the table. Keep in mind in Level D, your readers have worked hard to learn how to look at print. Support their new skill by removing any books that rely on patterned text.

	Breaking words into parts to solve unfamiliar words	Using print and meaning together	Reading with phrasing and intonation
New behavior	▪ Teacher writes the word on a white board and shows the parts. ▪ Teacher masks the parts with a cardboard mask, revealing each word part left to right.	▪ Prompt the child to reread the sentence with the tricky word, to refresh the context of the word in the sentence. "Start here and think about what's going to make sense. When you get to the tricky word, start the word right away."	▪ Teacher masks the text to show the groups of words in phrases, unmasking as the child reads each phrase. ▪ Teacher models what the dialogue should sound like. ▪ Explicitly teach what to do when a reader encounters a comma, period, question mark, and exclamation mark.
Inconsistent behavior	▪ "Where can you break it?" ▪ "What do you know about that word?" ▪ "Show yourself the parts."	▪ "You were using the letter sounds, now start again and also think about what would make sense." ▪ "You were thinking about what would make sense, and now go back and use the letters to make sure it looks and sounds right."	▪ Mask phrases and prompt, "Read these words altogether." ▪ "Make it sound like they would say it." ▪ "Try that again and use the commas."
Almost secure behavior	▪ "What can you try?" ▪ "Are you right?"	▪ "Are you right?"	▪ "How did you sound?"

FIGURE 6.10

Summary Table of Teaching with Level D

Learning High Frequency Words

In Level D, readers are continuing to expand the number and types of high frequency words they recognize automatically. **Sight words**, or words known by sight, serve a couple of important functions here. We know readers will need to slow down occasionally to solve some of the new, more complex words that appear in Level D and beyond. We don't want them also slowing down trying to remember or decode high frequency words or words that could be committed to memory. A second benefit of learning a wide variety of types of sight words is using those words as links to solving new words with the same spelling patterns. When a child knows a high frequency word with a particular long vowel pattern, for example *like*, this will make reading other words with that vowel pattern easier. Sometimes it's good to take stock of your children's personal high frequency word sheets (see Figure 6.11) and look for evidence of a variety of spelling patterns. If you see a gap and know of a word that might fill that gap and appears in their reading or writing, this can guide your teaching. For example, the chart in Figure 6.12 seems to lack any words with a short *e* vowel pattern. Perhaps learning the word *get* or *let* might be a good word for this child.

When deciding which words to teach, you'll want to examine the books you use and make sure you are teaching the high frequency words that give your children the greatest chances to monitor. You also have to consider your school's adopted curriculum. If the word list adopted by your curriculum doesn't match the books your children are reading, continue to make sure you teach the words your readers need to monitor in the books they read!

Continue teaching and practicing high frequency words (see Chapter 5, pages 104–107) after reading books in each lesson and during the writing portion of the lesson. Occasionally

a	b	c	d	e	f	g
a and at		cat can	dad dog			go
h	**i**	**j**	**k**	**l**	**m**	**n**
	I is it			like look	mom me my	no
o	**p**	**q**	**r**	**s**	**t**	**u**
on	play			see	to	up
v	**w**	**x**	**y**	**z**		
	we		you	zoo		

FIGURE 6.11

Example Personal High Frequency Word Chart

check this learning, returning to previously taught words, just to make sure. Children are building a foundation here, so it needs to be firm.

Word Study

As we progress into Level D texts, we shift our learning goals in word study to match the texts the children read. So, we start including digraphs, consonant clusters, and simple analogies into the work with magnetic letters and sound boxes. We describe below some sample activities. Refer to Chapter 5, pages 107–113 for a complete introduction to these activities. Use your own ideas and the needs of your groups to design your word study activities.

In general, we stick with two basic types of activities: using magnetic letters to build words and writing words in sound boxes. Both activities allow children to listen for the sounds in words and link them to letters or letter clusters. They also allow you to reverse the process and have children look at letters or letter clusters and link them to sounds.

When using magnetic letters, have the needed letters quickly available, either in baggies or on magnetic trays. Some teachers prepare individual trays ahead of time. Others have students select the needed letters during the lesson. Both approaches can work if you are organized and have prepared your students well for the routine, but you need to use time very efficiently.

Learning Goal 1: Use Digraphs and Consonant Blends to Solve Words in Reading and Writing

Make Words with Magnetic Letters

1. Select some words from the spelling patterns outlined in Figure 6.12, or other similar words that follow the spelling pattern. Provide the needed magnetic letters. When you introduce this activity, you may wish to start with some words they have encountered in their books or their writing.
2. Say the word for the children. Have the children say the word slowly to hear each sound.
3. Each child makes the word with their magnetic letters and then checks their word by running their finger under it, matching the sounds they say to the letters they see.

Digraph–Vowel–Consonant	Consonant Blend–Vowel–Consonant	Consonant–Vowel–Digraph	Consonant–Vowel–Consonant Blend
that	clip	with	last
this	clop	moth	mist
chat	stop	wish	mask
chip	grab	dish	gasp
shot	slip	fish	wisp
shut	plop	lash	held

FIGURE 6.12

Sample Words for Word Study in Level D

Use Sound Boxes to Write Words

1. Provide predrawn sound boxes for each child. (See Chapter 5, pages 111–112.)
2. Say the word for the children. Have the children say the word slowly to hear each sound.
3. Children write in the sounds, left to right, from beginning to end.
4. Children check their word, by running their finger under it, matching the sounds they say to the letters they see.

Learning Goal 2: Use Analogy to Solve Simple Words

Using analogy to solve new words is a rather complicated skill. It's not unusual to think it's easier than it is and mistake being able to list rhyming words or chant rhyming with being able to apply the concept to reading new words. It is, however, a skill that can aid in efficient word solving, as Goswami and Bryant showed in their research (1990). In Level D, children will be beginners, so we plant the beginning seeds for this skill.

Look for signs that children are proficient at monitoring and using first letters to read. Look for signs they are looking at words beyond the first letter and blending simple CVC words. Look for signs they can hear and recognize rhyming words. These are all signs they are ready to use analogy to solve new words.

For the first lessons, model. The children will not have their own magnetic letters yet. Call on them to watch you, help you move your letters, and say the sounds with you. When you feel you have modeled enough, you can start having them use their own letters.

1. Provide the needed magnetic letters to make three or four words.
2. Start with a known word from one of the books you've read. Choose a word with a very simple rime. Examples include *cat, like, stop, no.*
3. Break the onset of the known word to the left and read the word: *l . . . ike.*
4. Ask, "What letter do we need to make *like* into *mike?*" (It's easier at first if the first letters represent **continuous sounds** or sounds the children can elongate and really hear and think about. These letters include *m, s, l, r, n, v, z,* and *h.*
5. Change the first letter. Children check their word, by running their finger under it, matching the sounds they say to the letters they see.
6. Do a couple of these. Then tell the children to change the first letter to a letter of your choosing. This will now become a reading task.
7. Have the children break the onset, make the sound, and then add the rime, reading the new word.
8. Have them do their best to read in a quiet whisper voice if possible so everyone gets a chance to discover the new word on their own. If this doesn't work out, give every other child a different first letter, so everyone gets a chance to do the reading on their own.

Writing

As you enter text Level D with your readers and writers, most of the writing responsibility has shifted to the student. Your focus will no longer be on directionality, managing space, and return sweep because these writing behaviors have become automatic. You will, however, continue to grow every child's writing vocabulary. A natural benefit of reading and writing more texts along with the increasing level of text complexity is acquiring more and more words at a faster pace. You will also be providing instruction on how to hear and link sounds to write more complex words.

The writing focus in text Level D shifts to comprehension. Instead of a carefully teacher-crafted text, as in the earlier text Levels Pre-A to C, what a child decides to write about will evolve from the conversations the small group has after reading the book. Of course, you can help steer that conversation with your book choice. Will you choose a fiction book or a nonfiction book? (The conversation will sound much different depending on your choice.) Regardless, make sure to expose children to both types of texts so they gain experience writing about each.

Before Writing

Once you have made that very important book choice, fiction or nonfiction, you will need to craft the beginning of the discussion by thinking of your comprehension goal. With a Level D fiction book, we encourage you to focus on either the story sequence or the problem and solution. So, you might begin the conversation with these questions:

- *How did this story begin? What happened in the middle of the story? How did the story end?*
- *What was the problem in this story? How did it get solved?*

With a nonfiction book, we encourage you to focus on learning facts about the book topic or focusing on the steps in a "how to" book. So, you might begin the conversation with these questions:

- *What did you learn about (topic)?*
- *What were the steps taken to get from the beginning to the end of the process?*

You will want to make sure your questions lead to a rich discussion that encompasses fictional or nonfictional language and vocabulary depending on the type of book your group reads. In some cases, you might have to prompt with more guiding questions to draw out that book language and vocabulary. After the discussion, children will decide for themselves what they will write about the book. Before they get started, we encourage you to check in with each student and have them tell you about what they plan to write so you can make sure they are on target with your comprehension goal.

Figure 6.13 take a closer look at what Mrs. Jones considers as she picks books for her small group's reading Level D fiction and nonfiction books.

During Writing

Now, at your small group table, you have three to five students all writing about the same book but expressing their thinking in possibly different ways. This can seem a bit hectic but the more practice you have the more natural it will begin to feel. As teachers, we have the unique knack of helping one student while still giving some attention to the other students at the table so we can home in when they need assistance too.

Knowing your students' writing abilities well will help you to know when to attend to each child and teach to each of their individual needs. Depending on the student, they might need to practice the following:

- A high frequency word several times to help build those neural pathways that lead to automaticity when writing it
- Rereading while writing to keep the meaning going and make sure their writing makes sense
- Hearing and recording sounds in sequence using sound boxes
- Breaking longer words into syllables to work on writing one syllable at a time

Fiction Book

Book	Beginning/Middle/End	Problem Solution
Where Is Big Cat?  Synopsis: When it's time for Mom to brush Big Cat, Big Cat runs to find a place to hide. After a little bit of looking, Big Cat finally finds the best place to hide.	What happens in the beginning of the story? <u>Possibilities:</u> 1. Mom wonders where Big Cat is so she can brush him. 2. Big Cat does not want Mom to brush him, so he goes to find a place to hide. What happens in the middle of the story? <u>Possibilities:</u> 1. Big Cat tries to hide in the tub but it is too wet. 2. Big Cat tries to hide in a box but it is too small. 3. Big Cat tries a few hiding places but they are not good ones. What happens in the end of the story? <u>Possibilities:</u> 1. Big Cat sees a toy cat and gets a great idea of where to hide. 2. Big Cat hides in the toy box with the stuffed animals.	What problem did Big Cat have? <u>Possibilities:</u> 1. Big Cat did not want to be brushed by Mom, so he had to find a place to hide. 2. Big Cat can't find a place that is just right to hide from Mom. How did the problem get solved? <u>Possibilities:</u> 1. Big Cat tried several hiding places and finally found the perfect one in the toy box. 2. Big Cat hid from Mom in the toy box filled with stuffed animals.

FIGURE 6.13

Mrs. Jones's Fiction and Non-Fiction Book Picks for Her Small Group

Nonfiction Book

Title	Facts	How To
The Hot Rods Synopsis: This book is about old cars that are given a brand-new look.	What did you learn about hot rods? Possibilities: 1. Hot rods are old cars with a new look. 2. Hot rods come in many different colors. 3. Hot rods sometimes have flames on the side. 4. Hot rods have engines. 5. Hot rods can go fast.	How do you make a hot rod? Possibilities: 1. Get an old car. Fix it and paint it a cool color. Paint flames on the side. Drive it really fast! 2. Fix up and paint an old car. Put some flames on the car. Drive it really fast.

FIGURE 6.13   (*Continued*)

After Writing

Finishing writing in text Level D is not much different than in text Level C. Since children are composing their own thoughts about the book, they will, most likely, finish their writing at different times. It will continue to be important for students to reflect on how their writing sounds and how their writing looks. You might even consider creating a checklist with the children, outside of the small group table, that can be used during writer's workshop, literacy centers, and during small group to assist them with their reflection on their writing.

As always, if time permits, let the children to do a quick sketch of their writing. This sketch provides a visual reminder of what they wrote about the books they read at the small group table.

Remember to check out our correlating literacy center ideas that support the work students are doing at the small-group table with Level D texts.

www.stenhouse.com/content/intentional-from-the-start

REMEMBER THE PURPOSE OF TEACHING WITH LEVEL D TEXTS

To integrate means to bring together or unite separate things into a whole. Level D text provides opportunities for young readers to learn to integrate many features of literacy. They are uniting clusters of letters to make solving more efficient. They are merging print information with meaning information to ensure comprehension. They are bringing together meaningful groups of words to make their reading phrased, again ensuring comprehension. Like the swimmers we talked about at the beginning of this chapter, who were removing their floaties, our children no longer need the types of scaffolds we provided to get them started as readers. Swimmers without floaties integrate their movements, arms, and legs simultaneously, to stay afloat. Readers in Level D and beyond do the same thing, integrating many skills, to keep their reading afloat.

EXAMPLE LESSON WITH LEVEL D TEXTS

Mrs. Jones has planned this small group for E.J., Aubrey, and Will, who have been focusing their attention on Level D texts. She plans to introduce a new book titled *The Roller Coaster*. The story is about Carlos and Maria, who go to an amusement park with their father. Both of the kids want to go on the roller coaster and their dad agrees but in the end, he is sorry he did. During the two days of lessons Mrs. Jones will have students:

- Read familiar books with phrasing and fluency
- Read the new book
- Learn the high frequency word *then*
- Focus on the *th* digraph
- Write about what happened in the beginning, middle, and end of the story

Figure 6.14 gives you a glimpse into how Mrs. Jones's lesson might look and sound.

DAY 1

Component: Familiar Reading
Focus: Phrasing and Fluency

Mrs. Jones lays the books *Where Is My Cat?*, *Little Fox*, *Where is the Big Cat?*, and *Hot Rods* on the table so Aubrey, E.J., and Will can get started right away with familiar reading. She chooses these books because they are well loved by all three children and provide opportunities for them to practice phrasing and fluency.

As the children get started, Mrs. Jones is leaning in and specifically listening to how the reading sounds. Depending on what she hears, she might use these prompts:

- "Try that again and make it sound like you're talking."

- Cover up some of the words so only a two-to-four-word phrase is showing and say, "Can you put these words together like talking?"

- "Listen to me read it. Now you try it on the next part."

She notices E.J. is reading with a robot voice and decides to step in.

FIGURE 6.14
Example Lesson for The Roller Coaster

Student and Teacher Interactions

E.J. is reading *Hot Rods* (page 6).

E.J. (word by word): Here. . .are. . .two. . . no, three. . .hot. . .rods. One. . .is. . .blue. One. . .is. . .red. One. . .is. . .yellow. Hot. . . rods. . .come. . .in. . .a. . .lot. . .of. . .colors.

Mrs. Jones: E.J., you're using your robot reading voice again. Is this book about robots?

E.J.: No.

Mrs. Jones: You're right it's not. So, you should read it like you're talking. Let me show you how to put some of these words together in phrases.

Mrs. Jones (using the mask): Now put these words together like you're talking.

E.J.: Here are

Mrs. Jones: Good! Now put these together.

E.J.: three hot rods.

Mrs. Jones: Keep going!

E.J.: One is blue. One is red. One is yellow. Hot rods come. . .in a lot. . .of colors.

Mrs. Jones: That sounded great! Now go back and try that whole page again by yourself.

Teacher Moves and Rationale

Mrs. Jones decides to bring out a small strip of paper to mask some of the text. She will show E.J. one phrase at a time, down the page, and encourage him to put the words together so they sound like talking.

Mrs. Jones leaves E.J. to continue practicing phrased reading on his own while she turns to listen to Aubrey and Will. She praises Aubrey about how her reading sounds. She notices Will is still reading with a staccato voice. So, she decides to appeal to his eyes and ears by taking turns reading pages of the book with him. This will give him the opportunity to hear how the reading should sound while he still attends to the print.

Component: Introduce and Read New Book *The Roller Coaster*
Focuses: Monitoring with high frequency words and looking across a word to attempt to solve it using meaning, structure, and letter and sound information

---

Mrs. Jones has decided to introduce the book *The Roller Coaster*. She first sets the stage by tapping into the children's background knowledge about riding roller coasters. She then delves into how the characters in the book might be feeling about going on a roller coaster.

Student and Teacher Interactions

Mrs. Jones: Let's look at these pages. How do you think everyone is feeling about riding the roller coaster? What clues do you have?

Will: The kids look like they're having fun because they are smiling.

E.J.: And they're raising their hands up but dad is holding on.

Teacher Moves and Rationale

Mrs. Jones shows pages 10 to 14 in order to talk about how each person might be feeling.

Mrs. Jones hands out books one at time so she can make sure that everyone has a successful start. Then she begins listening in and supporting each child

FIGURE 6.14 (*Continued*)

Aubrey: Yeah, I don't think he's having fun. He might be scared.
Mrs. Jones: Or maybe he has a funny tummy like yours Aubrey.
Aubrey: (giggling) Maybe he's going to get sick.
Mrs. Jones: Well, you'll have to read the book to find out how dad feels.

Will: Can we go on it, Dad? said Carlos. Can we. . ./p/ /l/, /pl/, play? No that's not play. Can we /pl/ /e/ /a/ /s/ /e/, ple-a-see?
Mrs. Jones: Hmmm. Does that make sense?
Will: No.
Mrs. Jones: Ok, let's try it again. Start here (Can) and when you get to this word make the sound it starts with and think what would make sense with what Maria is asking.
Will: can we /pl/
Mrs. Jones (unmasks /ea/): This part is like "ea-t."
Will: /plea//s/, please!
Mrs. Jones: Good work. Now read that again so it all makes sense.
Will reads the rest of the page without difficulty.

Mrs. Jones: There was a word on page 5 that was a bit tricky for some of you. Let's look at how that word *please* works so you'll know how to solve new words that work like it. Watch me break off the first part. What sounds do you see?
Children: /pl/.
Mrs. Jones: Yes! *pl* says /pl/! Now this part works like this word "eat". What sound do these letters (*ea*) make in *eat*?
Children: /ea/.

as they read. She listens into Will first (page 3) and notices he is struggling with the word *please*.

Mrs. Jones masks the word *please* and shows just the *pl* so Will can get the word started.
Mrs. Jones knows *eat* is a known word for Will, so she chooses it to help him with the middle part of *please*.
As Mrs. Jones listens to the others at the table, she decides it's best not to interrupt Aubrey's successful reading. So, she turns to E.J. and assists him with his intonation and speed before bringing the group back together.

Mrs. Jones has a brief discussion about the book to check on the children's comprehension of the story and then jumps right into her teaching point.

FIGURE 6.14 *(Continued)*

Mrs. Jones: Good now let's put those two parts together.
Mrs. Jones and Children: /pl/ /ea/. . ./plea/.
Mrs. Jones: Now put it all together.
Children: Please!
Mrs. Jones: Go back to page 5 and point to the word *please*. Run your finger under it slowly as you read it.
Children: /pleeeeease/.
Mrs. Jones: Now read the whole page.

Again, Mrs. Jones knows it's important to put that hard work back into the continuous text to maintain the meaning of the story.

Component: High Frequency Word Practice
Focus: Learn a new high frequency word

Mrs. Jones starts the high frequency word practice with two well-known words, *the* and *this*. From this initial practice, she moves right into teaching the new high frequency word *then* because it begins with the digraph *th* just like *the* and *this* and she wants the children to begin to notice *th* is in many words they will read and write.

Student and Teacher Interactions
Mrs. Jones: What do you notice about words *the* and *this*?
Children: Both words start with a *th*!
Mrs. Jones: That's right! *The* and *this* both start with *th*. I am going to teach you another word that begins with *th*. Watch me write it on my board. Now, don't call it out if you figure the word out. Just put your finger on your nose to show you might be able to read it.

Teacher Moves and Rationale
Mrs. Jones writes *then* on the board in large letters. She anticipates that students will notice the *th* and the word part *en* and can put the parts together fast to read the new word *then*.

Mrs. Jones: E.J. you were thinking about it pretty hard. What did you notice about the word?
E.J.: I was thinking about the parts. I knew the *th* sound and the *en* part is in *hen* like on our vowel chart. So /th/ and /en/ together say *then*.
Mrs. Jones: What a great way to work that out E.J.! Now, everyone erase *the* and *this* and make the word *then* with magnetic letters on your board.

As Mrs. Jones finishes writing the word Aubrey and Will put their fingers on their nose fast. She waits to give E.J. a chance to work it out. *Then* was already a known word for Aubrey, and Will sounded out the word letter by letter. She asks E.J. to explain how he figured out the word.
Mrs. Jones finishes the high frequency word practice portion of the lesson by giving the children the opportunity to

FIGURE 6.14   (*Continued*)

build *then* with magnetic letters, write it on their white boards and locate it in their books.

Component: Word Study
Focus: Working with the digraph *th*

Mrs. Jones brings three trays with magnetic letters on them to make words that have the digraph *th* in them: *that, thank, thin, with, path, cloth.* She always prepares for more words than she thinks she'll need just in case the work is easy and goes fast.

Student and Teacher Interactions

Mrs. Jones: Well, now that you can read and write at least three words that have the digraph *th* in them, let's try building a few more! Listen to this word: *that.* Say it slowly.

Children: /thaaaaaaaat/.

Aubrey: I hear *at* in it like *cat* from our vowel chart!

Will: Me too!

Mrs. Jones: I do too! Knowing that will help you to build the word *that.* Say it again slowly and as you do, think about the sounds you hear and build the word with magnetic letters. Do you hear the /th/ at the beginning of the word or the end?

Children: Beginning!

Mrs. Jones: Now put your finger under the first part of the word and slide your finger slowly as you read the word *that.*

Children: thaaaaaaat

Mrs. Jones: Are you right?

Children: Yes!

Mrs. Jones: That word looks just the way it sounds! Ok, let's try another one: *thin.* Remember to say it slowly as you think about the sounds you hear and then build it.

Teacher Moves and Rationale

Mrs. Jones guides the children through the process of building the *th* words by having them:

- say the word slowly.
- listen for sounds in sequence from the beginning of the word to the end.
- build the word with magnetic letters.
- check the word by reading it slowly.

Mrs. Jones continues in this same manner until it's time to end the group lesson.

FIGURE 6.14 (*Continued*)

Student Name: _Will_____ Date: _____

Evidence of problem solving: _Some integration of errors._
Cross checked meaning and structure using
visual or visual with meaning and structure.
Used meaning and structure and neglected visual.

Page	Title/Level: The Roller Coaster	E	SC	E/Analysis	SC/Analysis
2	"Look, Dad," said Carlos. / at/sc Dad / T	1		m s ⓥ	m s ⓥ
	"Here is the roller coaster."				
	Wow! said Maria. / Whoa		1		m s ⓥ
	"That is a big roller coaster!"				
5	"Can we go on it, Dad?" said Carlos.	1		m s ⓥ	m s ⓥ
	"Can we, please?" said Maria. / ply	1		ⓜ ⓢ v	m s ⓥ
	Dad looked at the roller coaster. / at/sc all/sc				
	Then he looked at Carlos and Maria. / The	1		m s ⓥ	m s ⓥ
7	"Yes," said Dad.				
	"We can go on the roller coaster." / can't/sc				
	"Oh, thank you, Dad." / Won't/T	1		m s ⓥ	m s ⓥ
	said Maria and Carlos.				
8	Maria and Carlos				

Page		E	SC	E/Analysis	SC/Analysis
11	got into the roller coaster. / get	1		m s ⓥ	
	Dad got into the roller coaster, too. / get	1		m s ⓥ	
	The roller coaster went up.				
	and up, and up, and up. / up/sc	1		m s ⓥ	m s ⓥ
12	Then the roller coaster / the/sc	1		m s ⓥ	m s ⓥ
	went				
	down,				
	down,				
	down.				
15	"I liked riding / going	1		m s ⓥ	
	on the roller coaster."				
	said Maria.				
	"Me too," said Carlos.				
16	"Not me!"				
	said Dad.				

Began reading choppy and became
more fluent and phrased as he read.

FIGURE 6.15

Will's Running Record for The Roller Coaster. As you can see by her notes and coding, Mrs. Jones notices Will integrated (used meaning, language structure, and print information) some of his errors. These are the type of errors Mrs. Jones hopes to see more of as Will becomes a more strategic reader. Will also cross-checked some of his errors. For example, when he read at for Dad, he initially used meaning and language structure and then self-corrected using print (letters and sounds) information. When he read on for oh, he initially used print information (letters and sounds) but self-corrected using story meaning and language structure. When Will read riding for going, he only used meaning and language structure and ignored the print (letters and sounds) information. This is an error Mrs. Jones will want to go back to as a teaching point especially with the many integrated and self-corrected errors Will demonstrated as he read The Roller Coaster.

DAY 2

Component: Reread New Book *The Roller Coaster*
Focus: Fluency and phrasing; looking across a word to attempt to solve it using meaning, structure, and letter and sound information

Mrs. Jones begins the day 2 lesson by having the children read the new book from day 1. While children read, Mrs. Jones takes a running record of Will reading the book. She will be listening for an opportunity to move Will and the whole group forward in their strategic work with text. See Figure 6.15 on previous page to see Will's running record and his strategic work as he read.

Component: High Frequency Word Practice
Focus: Writing high frequency words fast

Mrs. Jones chooses to practice the high frequency words that have the diagraph *th* in them. She wants these words to become fast and fluent so there's no mental energy spent reading them or writing them. All three children can write the word *the* fast. When Mrs. Jones notices that Aubrey writes *this* by writing *is* first and then adds the *th* to the left of it, she stops Aubrey, erases the word, and reteaches the importance of left-to-right directionality across words. She steps in to help E.J. when she sees him struggle to write the word *with*.

Mrs. Jones: Erase your boards and try the word *with*. It has the *th* at the end of the word instead of the beginning.
E.J.: /w/ /i/ /th/. . ./w/, w. . ./i/, i. . ./th/, th. . .with.
Mrs. Jones: Take a good look at the word *with*, E.J. Think you have it in your head? (E.J. nods.) OK, erase the word and write it again fast.
E.J.: w, i, t, h, with.
Mrs. Jones: Nice job, E.J. Erase it and write it one more time fast.

Mrs. Jones notices that E.J. has to say the sounds in *with* before he writes it. She knows this is inefficient responding and prefers that he write *with* fast with less thinking about it. She encourages him to study the word and then write it again several times. She has him erase after each writing so he has to think about the word and recall it fast.

Component: Writing
Focus: Comprehending, organizing thoughts, and writing about the book; writing high frequency words fast; hearing and recording sounds in sequence when writing more complex words

FIGURE 6.14 (*Continued*)

CHAPTER 6

With the children, Mrs. Jones has a quick conversation about the events that happened in the beginning, middle, and end of *The Roller Coaster*. When she hands out their writing books, she shows the children how she has prepared the page like a graphic organizer with a separate space to write about the beginning, middle, and end of the story. She encourages E.J., Will, and Aubrey to compose their own writing and get started. As they write, she monitors their progress and provides support when they need assistance.

Student and Teacher Interactions	Teacher Moves and Rationale
(Mrs. Jones turns to check in with E.J. He has written "The kids beg dad to"). **Mrs. Jones:** E.J. would you like sound boxes for ride or do you think you can write it? **E.J.:** /r/ /i/ /d/. I can write it!	Mrs. Jones checks in with E.J. she knows he is good at hearing sounds in sequence. She offers him a choice of sound boxes but knows he can write *ride* without them.
Mrs. Jones: Ok. How are you doing Aubrey? Read what you have written so far. **Aubrey:** I don't know how to write the word *saw*. **Mrs. Jones:** I can help you. Here is the word *saw*. Write it here, here, here, and here. (Aubrey writes the word *saw* fast and continues with her writing.)	Mrs. Jones suspects Aubrey might need help writing *saw* so she checks in just as Aubrey gets to that word in her writing. Up on the practice page, Mrs. Jones writes the word *saw* because sound boxes don't work here. However, it's a word that Aubrey will be coming across more frequently in her reading and writing in Level D and beyond.
Mrs. Jones: Will, read me what you have written please. **Will:** The kids and dad go on the big. Roller is a big word. **Mrs. Jones:** It is, so clap it. **Will:** rol (clap) ler (clap).	When Mrs. Jones checks in with Will, he is getting ready to work on the word *roller*. She waits to follow his lead to know how to step in and scaffold his writing.
Mrs. Jones: What's the first part? **Will:** rol **Mrs. Jones:** Here are the sound boxes for that part. Say it slowly and write the sounds you hear. **Will:** /r/ r; /o/ o; /l/ l. (Will writes as he makes and links the sounds.)	Mrs. Jones decides to put *roller* in sound boxes one syllable at a time (*rol-ler*) right in the running text he is writing. Mrs. Jones uses this same process with E.J. but Aubrey has already solved it on her own when Mrs. Jones checks in with her again.

FIGURE 6.14   (*Continued*)

Mrs. Jones: Good, now clap and say the second part.

Will: rol (clap) ler (clap).

Mrs. Jones: Here are the boxes for the second part.

Will: /l/ l; /r/ r. (He writes as he makes and links the sounds.)

Mrs. Jones: Run your finger under the word and check it. Are you right?

Will: r-o-ll-er, yes!

When the children get to *coaster*, Mrs. Jones provides sound boxes if needed.

As the children finish with their writing about what happened in the beginning of the story, Mrs. Jones asks them what they will write about the middle of the story. She knows the children will have little difficulty writing about what happened in the middle of the story. So she leans back and watches them carefully. She prompts them occasionally to reread so they know what word they will write next.

Mrs. Jones repeats the same process of asking what the children will write for the end of the story and watches as they get started.

Aubrey decides to write: *The kids had fun on the roller coaster but dad got sick.*

Mrs. Jones knows this will all be easy and fast for Aubrey but she keeps an eye on her just in case.

Will decides to write: *Dad did not like riding the roller coaster.*

Mrs. Jones is prepared to jump in and help with the word *riding*. She will ask if he wants sound boxes or to try it without.

E.J. decides to write: *When they got off the roller coaster, dad felt sick.*

Mrs. Jones knows *felt* can be tricky because the /e/ gets swallowed and sounds like the letter *l*. So, she helps by giving him four sound boxes to help him separate the four different sounds.

As E.J., Will, and Aubrey finish their writing, Mrs. Jones acknowledges their hard work and gives them a minute or two to draw a quick picture.

FIGURE 6.14

Conclusion: It's Just the Beginning

As teachers of very young children, we've all experienced meeting someone outside our profession who doesn't quite get what we do. They look at us with the knowing smile, cooing "Oh, it must be so fun to teach little children and get to color and glue all day!" If you're like us, we never know whether to just smile back and say "Yes! It's so much fun!" or sit them down and try to explain the complex learning that happens, and the level of professional knowledge needed to achieve it. Though certainly misguided, these people aren't trying to offend—they just don't understand the complexity involved in what appears so simple.

The same can be said about the earliest levels of text. These books, which appear to be so simple and can be "read" so easily, are actually written in intricate, purposeful ways that support complex literacy skills with our youngest readers. Think back to teaching for one-to-one matching, for example. We talked about what could happen when teachers don't have a clear understanding of how to help children achieve a firm, automatic grasp of voice-to-print matching. They might allow their readers to quickly read through Levels A, B, and even C books, just relying on patterned text to say the right words. They might not know to use patterned text only as a scaffold for teaching directionality and one-to-one matching to children who have no footholds in print. They might not know how to remove the scaffold of pattern as they carefully build those print footholds and skills. They might not be carefully checking for finger, eye, voice, and print match in Pre-A, A, and B text. And unless teachers have a firm understanding of how to use these early-level books, problems will likely occur when their children get beyond early levels.

Just as a swimmer moving into the deep end too soon will likely need a rescue, so will a reader who hasn't shored up the needed skills in early levels. We would emphasize a couple of reminders in making sure your readers don't need a rescue as they move on from Level D. One is not to be fooled by patterned or easily memorized text. Early texts need some pattern, as we have talked about, but make sure your readers aren't still depending on language structure by the time they are reading in Levels C and D. They will sink quickly in higher levels if they aren't efficiently able to break words and use print information. Make sure all your teaching decisions lead to learning how to carefully use print while not losing meaning. Second, teach explicitly and clearly in early levels and then move on. As Reading Recovery™ trainer Mary Fried would tell teachers, "Don't stay too low too long." When you see evidence that your readers are ready to move out of the very simple early levels, expose them to the next bands of text levels, especially if you are a first-grade teacher. The next band of levels will still reinforce their current skills, but also expose them to more words, more opportunities to solve, and more complex stories.

From the start, when we first compose Pre-A text with our children, reading for meaning is always at the forefront of our guided reading lessons. As we move children into Level A texts, we always take great care in looking for books that offer the most appealing stories and topics for our children, so they can think about meaning as they read. The writing portion of the lesson is meaningful and connected to their reading. This is purposeful and based on Clay's original research (2005a and 2005b). Her research showed that young children who were making good progress in their literacy development considered meaning as they problem solved. We teach our children to consider meaning as well, while they are simultaneously learning to use the print information. Teaching children to consider meaning from the earliest levels also sets the expectation that readers monitor comprehension. Thinking while reading is rewarded by the enjoyment of these stories and informational books that appeal to their interests. It's a fact that we all do more of activities we enjoy. If our children find reading enjoyable because the books are funny or exciting or interesting, they are much more likely to do more of it. If they find characters they like, or can relate to, or can learn from, they are much more likely to read those books again and again. Falling in love with books (that you can read yourself) can start early if teachers are savvy book-choosers and know how to scaffold. We hope this never gets lost in the busyness of teaching for letters and sounds and words.

Clay (2005a, page 40) says a teacher's goal is to "aim to produce independent readers so that reading and writing improve whenever children read and write." She says when using text of appropriate difficulty, children begin to notice new aspects of print, monitor previously unnoticed mismatches, self-correct their own errors, and discover new things on their own. These behaviors are the beginnings of a *self-extending system*, or a system where the reader becomes more efficient and more competent "independent of the teacher." In other words, the reader begins to become a better reader by reading, and the writer begins to become a better writer by writing. Does this mean our children no longer need explicit instruction? Absolutely not! We have much, much more to teach, obviously! We are still in the early stages of literacy. But as in all learning tasks, there is much to be learned through independent practice. One of the beautiful aspects of guided reading is the teacher's opportunity to observe readers in the act of processing text. It is during these times of observation that you will likely notice evidence of the beginnings of self-extending systems in your readers. "Hey, that word looks like *cat*." Or, "No, wait, that can't be right!" Or, "Hey, I saw this word in a book at home!" All these are signs of new competencies initiated by the child. Take note, because these observations help you know how to scaffold as you move children into levels with more complexity.

As you move out of these early levels, your readers will now be ready for new reading challenges. The foundational skills should be firm and automatic, and you'll be looking for books that stretch your children's skills. Whether reading fiction or informational texts, the books will have more print with less picture support, more information to digest, more plot episodes to track, and longer words to read. This comprehension work requires fluency—not just "words per minute" fluency, but phrased, prosodic, accurate fluency. Your work in early levels on automaticity and accuracy with print and in phrasing has already set the stage for this. Your readers should already be putting meaningful groups of words together and already be monitoring every word as it contributes to their understanding of the story. This will set them up well for what's to come.

Your readers will also be ready to tackle books with more complex words, requiring more skill in decoding. You'll be looking for books in the next levels that provide just the right amount of challenge in decoding. The coming levels will require solving multisyllable words, using larger clusters of letters, and doing so quickly. Again, you've laid a strong foundation by teaching early for how to hear sounds in words, how to look efficiently at print, how to match sounds and letters, and how to break words into parts quickly. This careful scaffolding, and their intentional removal when it's time, beautifully sets up children to learn from Levels E and beyond.

Some of the most beautiful things are the simplest, and this is true about early-level books. Many are artfully written and provide a lovely reading experience for the novice reader to first dip their toe into print. We think these books are sometimes misunderstood and misused, and our goal with this book has been to shine a little light onto using them well, with the best outcomes for children in mind. By understanding the big purpose of each level and matching this directly to our students' needs, our teaching becomes precisely focused and we make it easier for our children to learn.

Every reading experience should bring joy, and we think that successful, early reading and writing interactions are especially important to that end. When children learn from the start, they can read for meaning while they use the print—they become thinking readers. How wonderful it is that this can start as early as Pre-A! We trust that this close look at small-group, guided reading instruction with your youngest readers will launch you and your children onto an ongoing, joyful literacy journey full of more and more challenging reading and writing experiences!

Professional Bibliography

Adams, Marilyn Jager. 1990. *Beginning to Read: Thinking and Learning about Print*. Cambridge, MA: MIT Press.

Allington, Richard L. 2012. *What Really Matters for Struggling Readers: Designing Research-Based Programs*. Boston, MA: Allyn and Bacon.

Bear, Donald R., Marcia Invernizzi, Shane Templeton, and Francine R. Johnston. 2019. *Words Their Way: Word Study for Phonics, Vocabulary, and Spelling Instruction*. Upper Saddle River, NJ: Pearson Education.

Clay, Marie M. 2001. *Change over Time in Children's Literacy Development*. Portsmouth, NH: Heinemann.

———. 2005a. *Literacy Lessons Designed for Individuals. Pt. 1, Why? When? And How?*. Portsmouth, NH: Heinemann.

———. 2005b. *Literacy Lessons Designed for Individuals. Pt. 2, Teaching Procedures*. Portsmouth, NH: Heinemann.

———. 2005c. *An Observation Survey of Early Literacy Achievement*. Portsmouth, NH: Heinemann.

———. 2015. *Becoming Literate: The Construction of Inner Control*. Portsmouth, NH: Heinemann.

Cunningham, Patricia. 1988. "Names: A Natural for Early Reading and Writing." *Reading Horizons: A Journal of Literacy and Language Arts* 28 (2). Retrieved from https://scholarworks.wmich.edu/reading_horizons/vol28/iss2/5.

Dolch, E. W. 1936. "A Basic Sight Vocabulary." *The Elementary School Journal* 36 (6): 456–460. https://doi.org/10.1086/457353.

Ehri, Linnea C., and Jennifer Sweet. 1991. "Fingerpoint-Reading of Memorized Text: What Enables Beginners to Process the Print?" *Reading Research Quarterly* 26 (4): 442. https://doi.org/10.2307/747897.

———. 2004. "Teaching Phonemic Awareness and Phonics: An Explanation of the National Reading Panel Meta-Analyses." In *The Voice of Evidence in Reading Research*, ed. Peggy McCardle and Vinita Chhabra. Baltimore, MD: Brookes Publishing.

———. 2013. "Orthographic Mapping in the Acquisition of Sight Word Reading, Spelling Memory, and Vocabulary Learning." *Scientific Studies of Reading* 18 (1): 5–21. https://doi.org/10.1080/10888438.2013.819356.

Elkonin, D. 1971. "Development of Speech." In *The Psychology of Preschool Children*, ed. A.V. Zaporozhets and D. B. Elkonin. Cambridge, MA: MIT Press.

Fisher, Douglas, and Nancy Frey. 2014. *Better Learning through Structured Teaching.* Alexandria, VA: ASCD.

Fountas, Irene C., and Gay Su Pinnell. 1996. *Guided Reading: Good First Teaching for All Children.* Portsmouth, NH: Heinemann.

Goswami, Usha, and Peter Bryant. 1990. *Phonological Skills and Learning to Read.* Essays in Developmental Psychology. Hillsdale, NJ: Lawrence Erlbaum.

Hattie, John. 2008. *Visible Learning: A Synthesis of over 800 Meta-Analyses Relating to Achievement.* London: Routledge.

Kress, Jacqueline E., and Edward Fry. 2016. *The Reading Teachers Book of Lists.* San Francisco, CA: Jossey-Bass.

Lyons, Carol A. 2003. *Teaching Struggling Readers: How to Use Brain-Based Research to Maximize Learning.* Portsmouth, NH: Heinemann.

Mcgee, Lea M., Hwewon Kim, Kathryn S. Nelson, and Mary D. Fried. 2015. "Change Over Time in First Graders' Strategic Use of Information at Point of Difficulty in Reading." *Reading Research Quarterly* 50 (3): 263–291. https://doi.org/10.1002/rrq.98.

National Institute of Child Health and Human Development (NICHD). 2000. *Report of the National Reading Panel: Teaching Children to Read: An Evidence-Based Assessment of the Scientific Research Literature on Reading and Its Implications for Reading Instruction: Reports of the Subgroups.* Washington, DC: NICHD.

Pinnell, Gay S., and Irene Fountas. 2017. *When Readers Struggle: Teaching that Works.* Portsmouth, NH: Heinemann.

Randell, Beverly. 1999. "Shaping the PM Story Books." *The Running Record* 11 (2): 1–6; 10–12. https://members.readingrecovery.org/members/secure/filearchive/file_secure_check.php?fid=48005949&fac=4426985&org_id=RRCN.

Rasinski, Timothy V., and Melissa Cheesman Smith. 2018. *The Megabook of Fluency: Strategies and Texts to Engage All Readers.* New York, NY: Scholastic.

Richardson, Jan. 2016. *The Next Step Forward in Guided Reading: An Assess-Decide-Guide Framework for Supporting Every Reader.* New York, NY: Scholastic.

Rosenblatt, Louise M. 1978. *The Reader, the Text, the Poem: The Transactional Theory of the Literary Work.* Carbondale, IL: Southern Illinois University Press.

Sims Bishop, Rudine. 1990. "Mirrors, Windows, and Sliding Glass Doors." *Perspectives* 1 (3): ix–xi.

Underwood, Benton J., and Leo Postman. 1960. "Extraexperimental Sources of Interference in Forgetting." *Psychological Review* 67 (2): 73–95. https://doi.org/10.1037/h004186.

Vygotski, Lev Semenovich, and Michael Cole. 1981. *Mind in Society: The Development of Higher Psychological Processes.* Cambridge, MA: Harvard University Press.

Zull, James E. 2002. *The Art of Changing the Brain: Enriching Teaching by Exploring the Biology of Learning.* Sterling, Va: Stylus.

Index